BEGINNER'S FIELD GUIDE TO RAISED BED, CONTAINER, AND VERTICAL GARDENING

HOW TO GROW EDIBLE PLANTS ANYWHERE!

HERBS * VEGETABLES * MICROGREENS

SADIE ROWSE

CONTENTS

INTRODUCTION

There is nothing better than sitting in the shade of a tree, enjoying a cool drink, and looking over the beautiful garden you have created. Gardening is one of the most fulfilling activities you can do. It gets you outside for some fresh air and vitamin D, a vitamin essential to strengthening bones and your immune system. It is also a great way to get exercise in as the digging, pruning, and carting away of garden waste can vary from light to heavy intensity exercise.

Gardening is a great bonding experience for the whole family, as each member can do something small to encourage the beautiful growth seen from spring to fall. Let's face it, is there anything quite as beautiful as a well-maintained garden? Whether you're growing trees and bushes to even your own vegetable patch, a healthy garden is filled with beauty and wonder.

Anyone can garden. It's an activity that helps to lower stress and anxiety while increasing your mood and satisfaction levels. It's even been known to help reduce feelings of anger. By actively gardening for 10 minutes or more a day, you lower your chances of a stroke or developing heart disease, and this isn't the only health benefit (IOL, 2020). By growing your own food, you lower the cost of your food bill, and you know exactly what went into growing your own vegetables. By using fewer pesticides, or using pesticides correctly, you get fewer toxins into your system. Also, the food you grow yourself always tastes better because you put the work and love into growing it. Gardening can even help bring out a creative side you never knew you had. Placing plants exactly where you want them ensures that you get the garden you always dreamed of.

However, what if you don't have space to have a garden? Are all these wonderful benefits lost to you? Are you doomed to stare at a tiny, empty plot of ground, with nothing to brighten your day? No! There are many ways to garden, and contrary to popular belief, you don't need a large piece of land to get the garden you want.

Even gardening small pieces of land will give you all the benefits of having a garden, you just need to be a little more space-savvy to achieve it. Small gardens with raised beds, balconies with containers, and even a small strip of ground in front of a wall are all you need to enjoy a garden. Raised bed, container, and vertical growing is your way to achieve that perfect garden to raise vegetables, microgreens, and herbs of all shapes and sizes! Don't have space outside? Don't worry! You can easily grow what you want inside, as long as you consider container size.

This book aims to put your fears of starting a garden at ease. Not only is it easy, but you will gain all the benefits of fresh vegetables and herbs. Within the following chapters you will find helpful hints about the basics of gardening in a raised bed, containers, and growing vertically, all with the end goal of utilizing what space and tools you have available to you.

By using these different growing strategies, you will soon find that you can grow whatever plants you wish with what space is available to you. While size matters in some regards, this isn't true for all forms of gardening! It's how you use the space you have and get the best from it.

When I was young, my family moved to a farm in Florida where we were able to raise cattle and work the land. This was where I got my love for gardening and understanding where our food comes from. As the years progressed, I realized there was no need to have a massive piece of land to grow what I wanted to eat. By controlling what I grew, I was able to take charge of my health in terms of diet and exercise.

This book is my way of showing others how easy it is to start your own garden wherever you live and with whatever space you have available and with next to no experience. Gardening is literally hands-on learning from season to season, and there is so much you can learn from year to year. You have to get your hands a little dirty to enjoy gardening, but it is worth the effort you put in and lots of fun!

By the end of this book, you will be able to make your own garden—whether it's raised beds, containers, or vertical growing space—care for it, and protect it from unwanted pests. The book is also full of handy tips to aid in creating the perfect, easily manageable garden to which you can return throughout the growing season to enjoy fresh crops. There is nothing difficult about gardening if you have the right information at your fingertips. By picking up this book, you have all the knowledge you need within its pages. There is no need to fear starting a garden when it is as easy as looking for the best location, the right soil, water, and some sunshine for either your seeds or transplants.

So, what are you waiting for? There are thousands of vegetables, herbs, and microgreens just waiting to be grown. Your garden is only limited by your imagination. Gardening starts with knowledge before a single seed or root gets placed in the dirt. Welcome to the wonderful world of raised beds, containers, and vertical growing gardens!

1

EASY AS 1, 2, 3! GARDENING BASICS

Before spending any money on starting your garden, you should consider what you need and how you will plan it out. Gardening is equal parts planning and digging in the dirt.

PLANNING

The first thing you need to do is ask yourself what you want from your garden. Certain plants grow better vertically than in a raised bed, while others prefer a raised bed to growing in a container. Not only that, but plant growth is dependent on the conditions around them. It isn't just water and sunshine that they need. Weather plays a vital role in how well your plants will grow. Frost, which comes too early or carries on longer than expected, tends to destroy gardens before you have even begun!

Start by making a list of your favorite edible plants and research whether they are easy to grow. Some plants need a little more care than others, so choose wisely. Once you know what you want to grow, you need to determine if they can grow where you are residing. However, don't let this limit you on what you choose to grow. What can't be grown outside can be grown indoors with a little help.

Hardiness Zones and Frost Dates

When considering growing outside, you have to think about how the hardiness zones can affect your garden. North America is divided into 13 hardiness zones. Each zone is determined by the average minimum winter temperature over the last 30 years. Zone 1 is the coldest of the zones from about -60 to -50 °F, while the warmest is Zone 13 at 60 to 70 °F. There is a 10 °F difference between each of the zones. These zones are also divided into subzones (Zone 1a and 1b), with a 5 °F difference between each subzone.

To determine what your hardiness zone is use the USDA Plant Hardiness Zone Map. Don't assume because your state has a specific zone, that you are in that zone. Some states can have up to three different zones! Not only are the zones governed by their own temperatures, but they also have their own frost dates.

These frost dates are when the first and last frosts will appear during the year. Frost will kill plants that aren't frost-tolerant, and if they aren't killed, their crops will be damaged beyond use. By knowing when these dates occur in your zone, you can determine when certain plants can be grown.

In the colder zones, there is a shorter growing period than in the warmer zones. This will have an impact on plants that require a longer growing season. Although this may limit you by what you can grow, you can use transplants (young plants) instead of seeds. This can save you a few weeks of growing time, lowering the duration the plant needs to reach maturity and produce crops.

Zones 10–13 generally don't have frost dates and are considered almost tropical, but that doesn't mean you can let your guard down. There is a chance that frost can sneak up on you, so always listen to weather warnings of frost. This will allow you to add extra protection to your plants.

Hardiness zones strongly affect plants that are grown outside. If you have a more sheltered area that can remain warmer, you may be able to extend your growing season by a few weeks when in a cooler zone.

Microclimates

Even if you are living in a certain zone, consider the microclimate of the area you are in. Microclimates are caused by the lay of the land, which can affect how much heat, wind, and moisture your local area receives. It can be difficult to determine what plants are best grown in your unique microclimate. So don't be afraid to get advice from other people in your area or ask for assistance at your closest garden center.

Bed Planning

Garden beds need to be planned out before planting! Some plants make great companions, while others will actively secrete chemicals to kill other plants (allelopathy). Not only that, but you can't grow the same plant in the same space year in and year out. Each plant needs a unique combination of minerals from the soil to get the best growth. If those minerals aren't replaced, then the next plant that needs those same minerals the following season will have less of them to use. This causes stunted growth and lower yield. To prevent this from occurring, a crop rotation system needs to be in place.

For crop rotation to work, a raised bed needs to be divided into sections where certain plants will grow per season. With each new season, a different crop needs to be rotated in while the old crops are rotated out. This will prevent minerals from being overused and a build-up of allelopathic chemicals.

Crop rotation is generally not required in container gardens as fertilizer is more readily added to it than in a raised bed. However, be wary of certain plants that can't be grown in the same place for several years, like potatoes.

Another reason to plan a bed is that some plants grow taller than others. As most plants require a minimum of six hours of sunlight, these tall plants can inhibit the growth of shorter plants if they cast too much shade over them. Planting taller plants to the north of the bed will prevent them from overshadowing those growing in the south, allowing all of them to get adequate sunlight.

Choosing the Right Plants

What you want to grow will affect how the raised bed is designed or how you will place your containers. Not only are some plants taller than others, but some need a little more support and require a trellis system.

Like people, plants do better with companions, but it is important to know which plants make good partners. Practicing companion planting helps increase plant yields, protects from pests, and encourages beneficial insects to visit your garden. It's also a good idea to research which plants go well together before planting.

Another thing you need to consider is whether you want to plant seeds or use transplants. Herbs such as rosemary are better planted as transplants as the seeds have a low chance of germinating under the wrong conditions. However, carrots are better planted as seeds as once the delicate root is damaged, the carrot grows poorly and will appear stunted or gnarled.

Growing from seeds or transplants has its own advantages and disadvantages depending on what plant you are trying to grow. Growing from seeds offers more of a variety to what you can plant. Some seeds are more tolerant of frost than transplants. However, other seeds require more work—such as soaking for a few hours before planting, as seen with peas. The seed you buy can also be too old to germinate, so check the seed packet before you purchase it. Lastly, growing from seed doesn't guarantee a seedling, whereas a transplant does. When growing in a location with a shorter growing season, transplants can give you several weeks' head start in comparison to planting seed. Luckily, if there is a particular variety of plants you want to grow in a colder zone. The only thing you need to do is start the seeds indoors and then plant out the transplants later in the season when the fear of a late frost has passed.

LOCATION

All plants are unique in their needs beyond sunlight and water. Some prefer to grow in cooler temperatures, while others prefer to be in full sunlight. Where you decide to place your garden will affect what you are able to grow.

When choosing a location, look for an area that is readily noticed. Having your garden within view encourages you to look in on its development daily. This helps you notice problems quickly and allows you to deal with them before they become disastrous.

This location needs to have access to a minimum of six hours of sunlight every day but may need more if the plants you are growing need more sunlight. Together with water, plants need light to undergo photosynthesis to grow. No sunlight means no growth and development, resulting in stunted growth and no crops produced.

The size of the bed you are planning needs to be carefully considered as you want to be able to reach all parts of it without having to step into it. The size of the bed will be dependent on the size of the property you have to work on. If you have the space for multiple raised beds or containers, ensure that you have enough space to move between them as you water, weed, and pick the produce.

Lastly, the location you pick to grow your garden must be in an area that you can protect from pets, pests, and even children. These critters can easily get into your garden and cause havoc if you don't keep an eye on them. Depending on what pests may be in the vicinity, especially the larger kind such as deer, you may have to protect the area with a fence.

WATER AND WATERING STRATEGIES

Don't have the location of your garden too far away from the water source you plan to use. No one wants to carry a heavy watering can to and fro from the tap. If the only place you can place your garden is far from a water source, consider laying your own drip irrigation system. This works particularly well with a raised bed.

Be wary of overwatering plants, as it can cause root rot if the soil is too wet. Watering from above can also pose a threat to the foliage (leaves) of the plant. Standing water and high humidity are the perfect breeding grounds for fungal infections such as downy and powdery mildew.

There needs to be a perfect balance between when and how much you water your garden. This is especially true for plants that require more water than others. The soil type you use will also affect how much water will be retained. Soil that is high in organic matter allows the water to drain well but also retains moisture better than sandy soils.

Contrary to popular belief, plants don't need to be watered daily if they receive adequate watering once or twice a week. Most plants like to receive an inch of water a week, though some may need more. To test whether the soil contains enough water, use a trowel or your finger, and dig down 2–3 inches. The soil should remain moist but not wet.

Many people favor using a hose when watering a garden. STOP! The force of the water can cause damage to the foliage and roots of young plants. It is better to use drip irrigation or a gentle sprinkle from a watering can to prevent damage.

SOIL AND SOIL CARE

Most soils found in gardens are old, and many essential minerals have long since leached from them. For raised beds and container gardens, avoid using the naturally occurring soil from a garden if you can help it. Not only can this soil be of poor quality, but it can also contain pests and soil-borne diseases that can be carried over into the smaller gardens.

Container gardens require nothing more than a potting mixture, but this isn't good enough for a raised bed garden. A raised bed needs a combination of organic matter (older compost) and potting soil mixture. If you have some good quality loamy soil, this can be worked into the mixture as well. Alternatively, talk with someone from your garden center about what is best to use in your raised bed. You want a well-aerated mixture that has no stones and can retain moisture.

Once the mixture is made, you will need to test the pH. Most plants like a slightly basic to neutral pH. If the pH is too low (acidic), you can add some lime, while if it is too high (basic), the pH can be lowered by adding some peat moss.

CONTAINER GARDENING

Whether you choose raised bed or container gardening, the choice comes down to the space available. With enough space, you can do both or either, it is completely up to you. However, when choosing to garden in containers, what containers you use is important.

Firstly, the size does matter as some plants need more room to produce something edible. You wouldn't grow potatoes in a gallon tub, but you can in something larger. Generally, container gardening isn't as physically intensive as raised bed gardening and is best used when you don't have a lot of space. By using some bricks and planks, you can create multiple levels for your containers to grow whatever and wherever you want. Remember to place the taller plants more to the north to prevent their shade from falling over the shorter plants.

The material the container is made of can also play a role. A lighter-colored material won't absorb as much heat as a darker-colored material. Clay and ceramic pots are lovely, but if the zone is too cold, there is a chance that they can freeze and even crack. It is cheaper, in the long run, to use food-grade plastic tubs to grow your produce in. Yet this doesn't stop you from using clay pots if you want to if you have them lying around.

The main thing to remember about using containers to garden is that they need to have drainage holes in them. With no drainage holes, water can gather at the bottom leading to the soil becoming anaerobic (lack of free oxygen). This, in turn, can cause serious damage to the plant's roots as they require oxygen to maintain their health.

GROWING UP: TO STAKE OR NOT TO STAKE

Vertical growing saves a lot of space and can be done against gates, walls, or along trellises. There are many kinds of plants that creep along the ground as they grow—including squash, cucumbers, etc. These plants take up a lot of space in a raised bed and are prone to soil-borne diseases and pests. By encouraging their growth upwards, you save a lot of space and prevent many different kinds of diseases and attacks from pests on the ground.

By growing vertically, you can better plan rows in a raised bed. This will allow you to increase your yield exponentially in comparison to allowing these plants to grow along the ground.

Even plants such as beans, peas, and tomatoes benefit from the support offered by trellises. This support allows the plant to produce more vegetables and fruit while not buckling under their weight. By trellising a plant that normally sprawls over a large area, you use less space for more yield. Trellising can be as inexpensive and as creative as what you have lying around, but more on that later.

MULCH

As with a regular garden, mulch should be added once the plants are a little older. When using mulch, you lower evaporation from the soil, deter some insect species, and prevent weeds from taking root and getting the sunlight they need to survive. With the prevention of evaporation, the plants become less stressed and therefore less susceptible to attack by pests. There are a variety of natural (shavings, grass, bark, etc.) and artificial mulch (rubber, plastic, glass, etc.) available. Typically, mulch should be 2–3 inches deep. Mulch less while plants are younger and add more as they get older.

FERTILIZER

Many people believe that the more you fertilize, the better the plant will do. Not only is this wrong, but this attitude can cause your plants to suffer. Fertilizing is dependent on what the fertilizer contains and when you decide to use it. Adding fertilizer to your raised beds and containers before you grow anything in it makes for healthier soil. However, overfertilizing will harm your plants (fertilizer burn), which results in either a damaged plant or one with a changed growth pattern.

Fertilizing too early can cause fertilizer burns to the roots and young leaves. However, fertilizing too late in the growing season can cause the plant to produce more foliage than blossoms, leading to a lower yield but a larger and greener plant.

The best way to handle fertilizing is to add light dosages to the plants two weeks after transplants have been added to the soil. This gives the plant time to adjust to its new environment. A slower and steadier diet of nutrients from the fertilizer allows for better root growth, allowing the plant to produce more blossoms and therefore more fruiting crops.

Before using any fertilizer, read the instructions to get the best results. Fertilizers can be bought in liquid or solid forms, and each should be applied differently. All additions of fertilizer should be halted as soon as the first blossom appears. This will help the plant to use its energy for producing crops rather than using it for growing.

TOOLS REQUIRED

Not all the tools suggested here may be something you want to use or may even need. However, to ensure the best gardening experience, it is a good idea to look at these tools as an investment rather than a frivolous purchase. Quality tools last for years, and when maintained well, it's a purchase you will hopefully only have to do once during your gardening adventure.

When container gardening, look for the size and color that will best suit your needs. Containers, unlike raised beds, mostly rely on potting soil to grow plants in. Be sure to purchase good potting soil so the plants are never in want of anything. A plant in a container should never become root bound, but it can if the nutrients in the soil are lacking and it needs to search for more. When working over a large area where you can have multiple raised beds, it can become tiresome to carry all the pots and trays of seedlings. A wheelbarrow can help with this back-breaking labor. It can also be used to mix your own organic-rich soils you want to use in your container or raised bed gardens. Although not a necessary piece of equipment, it is something that will make your life easier.

A small trowel will make it easier to dig holes to add transplants in, as well as to check how deep water has soaked into the raised bed. For raised bed gardening, you may need to get a larger shovel, hoe, and digging fork to help prepare the ground before the raised bed is added to your garden. It is always best to lay a raised bed on level ground. A large rake will also come in handy after your first successful growing season when you want to clear the bed of any remaining plant debris.

A watering can or a garden hose with a sprinkler head attachment is perfect for gently watering container gardens. They can also be perfect for a raised bed if you have no interest in installing drip irrigation.

Be sure to get some gardening gloves! Many plants have ways to protect themselves from animals that want to eat them, and this includes you. Gloves will protect your hands from even the most prickly leaves or vegetables.

Consider what extra assistance the plants you want to grow may need. If you are growing vertically, ensure you have stakes or trellises that can support the plant and its produce as it grows. Be as creative with this as you want.

Lastly, consider purchasing a sharp pair of gardening shears. When harvesting from a plant that produces throughout the season, you want to avoid damaging it as much as possible. By tearing away leaves or fruit, you leave behind a jagged wound that becomes susceptible to bacterial and viral infections that can kill your plant. A clean cut is less likely to be a breeding ground for diseases.

EASY GROWTH

No one is born knowing how to garden. It takes a lot of studying to get the perfect garden. However, there are almost foolproof, easy-to-grow plants that are perfect for beginners to try. If you have had a veggie garden before, you likely already know this, but if you are new, have a look at the list below to see which plants are best to start with.

However, before you get started, here are some handy tips for you. When deciding on a plant to grow, read the seed packet. It contains valuable information about when, where, the depth, and distances from other plants the seeds need to be planted. This is particularly important when planting in a raised bed. Secondly, consider the type of plant you are growing. Some are once-off when one seed produces a single crop—as seen with radishes, carrots, turnips, etc. These types of plants can be planted multiple times within a growing season. Other plants may produce several vegetables or leaves throughout their growing season—as seen with lettuce, chard, pumpkins, herbs, etc. These types of plants are always planted at the beginning of the season and are harvested throughout the time they grow.

FRUITS

There are several fruits perfect for a beginner, some of which need little attention to flourish. Botanically the plants below are considered fruit, but culinary-wise, people think of them as vegetables.

Peppers

Peppers, also known as capsicum, have many colors, shapes, and sizes you can plant in your garden— including bell peppers and a wide variety of chili peppers. While the bell peppers do well when given some support, chili peppers generally don't need much. Peppers can be grown in many different types of gardens, although the larger peppers will need to be supported once the fruit starts to develop.

Zucchini

Zucchini is a summer favorite for those who enjoy squashes. This plant can be grown sprawling or vertically and is best started from seed. Both the fruit and the flowers are edible. However, this plant requires a lot of water and warmth to give the best yields. You are spoiled for choice when it comes to shapes, sizes, and colors. It can be enjoyed raw in a salad or cooked in a stew.

Cucumbers

Cucumbers love the heat and will suffer if caught in an early frost. It will also quickly produce fruit if you have multiple plants growing in your garden. These fruits rapidly swell with water, so be sure to constantly water the plant while it is hot. The plant has easily recognizable male and female flowers. The female flowers—which have a tiny cucumber at the end of them—open at a different time than the male flowers. To have a good harvest, it's a good idea to stagger your planting so that there are always male and female flowers ready to be pollinated by beneficial insects. There are a variety of types you can plant, some of which are better in salads, while others make the perfect pickle. You can even consider planting the visually appealing lemon cucumber, which tends to be sweeter than other cucumbers.

Tomatoes

Tomatoes come in all shapes and sizes and are related to potatoes, peppers, and deadly nightshade. This fruit is easy to grow either as sprawling creepers or growing up trellises. They are perfect for any type of garden. If saving the seed for the following years, ensure that you are purchasing heirloom seeds that have a good track record for the yield you desire. Play around with cherry, Roma, and even Cherokee purple to see which variety grows best in your chosen garden.

VEGETABLES

There are many types of vegetables that vary from edible leaves, roots, or stems. Vegetables rarely need to be staked or encouraged to grow upwards. Depending on which type you want to grow, you may need more space above or below ground. Space appropriately.

Lettuce

Lettuce is a fast-growing plant—some as quick as 30 days to reach maturity—that prefers cooler temperatures. You can either wait for the plant to reach the end of its growth period before picking it, or you can help yourself to a few outer leaves now and again for a fresh salad whenever you want. Many varieties (cultivars) differ in taste, shape, color, and nutritional value. This plant can easily be grown in either a raised bed or container. However, lettuce is easier to grow from transplant than seed.

Swiss Chard

Similar to lettuce, Swiss chard can be enjoyed at the end of the harvest period or you can take a few leaves now and again. Swiss chard is known for its beautiful colors that will not only brighten your garden but also your plate. This plant likes warmth and water and will quickly wilt if you are hit with an extended heatwave.

Radish

Radish may be too peppery for some people, but it is a wonderfully easy vegetable to grow. It goes from seed to harvest in about 30 days or less, depending on the variety you want to grow. The root can be served fresh in a salad, or it can be pickled. The fresh green leaves can be added to a salad if you want to add extra taste to a low sodium diet.

Carrots

Carrots are a root vegetable that prefers cooler temperatures, which is great when they not only grow below ground but also under a canopy of leaves that cool the ground they grow in. Carrots can be grown throughout the year if you can keep them cool and don't suffer from frost. When you picture this classic vegetable, you likely see the orange vegetable which rabbits go crazy for. However, this vegetable comes in an array of colors and sizes to suit everyone's needs. For the best growth, ensure the soil this vegetable grows in has no clumps of soil or rocks, as this will prevent the root from developing correctly.

Beans

With beans, not only do you have trellis and bush varieties, but you also have varieties bursting with color, lengths, and flavors. This vegetable is a legume, and that means a plant source of protein, perfect for those living a vegetarian or vegan diet. Whichever variety you prefer to grow, know that it will need the support of some type of trellis, creating a lot of shade in your bed. Location is key when growing beans. Although possible to grow in a container, this plant will likely do best in a raised bed where it can spread out and produce many pods full of beans.

HERBS

Herbs differ from fruits and vegetables as only the leaves, seeds, or flowers are used in the flavoring of food. A single herb generally won't make up most of a meal, as seen with lettuce, and this is why lettuce isn't considered an herb, although its leaves are used. There are a wide variety of herbs you can grow from seed or transplant. The majority of them are easier to grow from transplant though. Herbs make great companion plants and attract many beneficial insects. However, some are highly allelopathic or have an invasive root system. Do your research before just planting anything you want. Herbs are great either in containers or in a raised bed.

Basil is a great herb that can be cooked fresh or dry and can be planted either from a seed or a transplant. It is the perfect companion to tomatoes as it keeps away tomato hornworms. Not only that, but the two plants are ideal for that perfect pasta sauce.

These are hardly the only plants you can grow, but they are the best for beginners. There are thousands of herbs, microgreens, and vegetables you can choose from. However, before you put seeds or transplants in the ground do your research! It isn't just the hardiness zone you need to be wary of. Some plants make great companions while others don't.

Take **mint**, for example. Great in a tea, perfect for attracting pollinators, but a terror in a raised bed. Mint spreads with its extensive root system, and it will only take a few good weeks during summer for it to completely take over your raised bed. Mint is best kept in a container—or a container added to a raised bed—if you want all the benefits it offers to your health and the health of your garden.

2

WHY USE A RAISED BED GARDEN

A raised bed is a garden bed placed over an existing piece of garden or flat structure. This bed is then filled with fertile soil and used as an extension of an existing garden or to create a new garden where there wasn't one before. Raised beds are not a container type of garden, as the bottom part is completely open and in contact with whatever it's placed on.

ADVANTAGES AND DISADVANTAGES

There are many advantages to having a raised bed garden in favor of a regular garden. The first is that it's perfect for someone who may not change the property (dig, till, etc.) they want to garden on, or if they don't wish to disturb the roots of trees and shrubs. If the soil condition is terrible, a raised bed offers an opportunity to garden with fertile soil you bring in. The raised bed, depending on the height, is ideal for someone who doesn't want to stoop or crouch to do gardening. You can even add a lip to the sides of the raised bed allowing you to sit comfortably on it.

You can determine how much soil is needed per bed once you have decided on the size you want to use. Unlike a garden where you need to mark out walkways, these can be designed around the raised beds, allowing you to move freely from one bed to the next. Although some may consider walkways a waste of space, they can be utilized with a trellis system that arches over them.

You don't need to spend a lot of money on constructing a raised bed. Depending on what you want to use, you can find materials that are being sold at reduced prices or even being given away. The design of a raised bed is only limited by the materials you use to make it from and your imagination. Raised beds can be aesthetically pleasing without spending a fortune.

By growing above the natural soil, the soil in the raised bed isn't as directly affected by the dampness and cold. It drains better and takes longer to get cold than the ground under it. You can control the health and type of soil you use in the bed. With the bed raised closer to eye level, you will notice infestations before they become a problem.

However, not everything is perfect with a raised bed, and there are some disadvantages. The size of the bed, especially the height, can drive up the cost of the construction materials as well as the cost of the soil needed to fill it. Because the raised beds drain so well, regular watering and mulching are a necessity to keep a healthy bed that can produce a high-yielding garden.

Raised beds have a finite life span, especially those made of wood. Not only that, but making a more permanent raised bed can become a problem if you wish to move away one day. It is important to consider the materials you want to use to make a raised bed.

DESIGNING A RAISED BED

As with planning a garden, it's in your best interest to design your raised bed on paper before you purchase anything. If possible, see how many of the materials you may need to build the raised bed you can pick up for free versus buying.

Size

The first thing you need to determine is the size of the raised bed you can place on your property. This is dependent on your property size and the materials you have access to. The most important part of the raised bed dimensions is the width. When sitting along the longer edges, you should be able to reach the center of the bed without stepping onto the soil. This ensures that you can adequately water and weed as needed without damaging plants and the soil structure underfoot. The best width is 3–4 feet across.

The length of the bed is determined by how much space you have available to you. As long as you stick to a 3–4 feet width, the length isn't a problem. With a width of four feet, it allows you to fit more rows of plants into your raised bed. The width is more important than the length. When considering multiple raised beds, it is a good idea to consider where your walkways will be and what their dimensions will be.

You will also need to consider what kind of raised bed you want to make when it comes to the height of the bed. When making a mound raised bed—a long mound of soil with some rocks along the edges to keep the soil in place—it can be 4–8 inches high and as long as 15 feet. However, this isn't high enough to grow larger plants but is perfect for herbs. When wanting a higher raised bed, you will need to consider one with raised and supported sides. These sides can be made from a multitude of sturdy materials and can measure from

10–18 inches deep. This is a comfortable height to sit and work from for most people.

The depth is important for root vegetables and plants that have extensive root systems. You want to avoid your plants becoming root-bound. This is when the plant is forced to send its roots out looking for water or nutrients but is unable to because it doesn't have enough space to grow. The deeper the roots need to go, the higher the supporting walls and the more volume of soil you will need to fill the bed. Generally, the growth you see above the soil mirrors the growth below.

Most people prefer to make a raised bed that is 4 x 8 feet with a depth of 10 inches. That isn't to say you have to stick to this! Your raised bed can be square, circular, or even a triangle tucked away in the corner of your garden; let your imagination run free with the space you have. The higher the bed stands, the more money it will cost to make and fill, unless you are lucky enough to have access to the necessary materials for free.

Location

The location of where you build your raised bed is important. Once it is built, especially a wooden raised bed, it becomes too difficult to carry it to where it is needed. Select a place in your garden that gets adequate sunlight and can easily be seen from your home. Be wary of having raised beds in the lower part of the garden. Although this can help with getting water to the bed through the use of gravity, it can also be a catchment area for rainwater to stand when there are storms. You will also need to consider other environmental effects such as wind, as this can rip blossoms from the plants, preventing a high-yielding crop.

When placing a raised bed on an uneven surface, it will need to be leveled and cleared of growth. Grass and weeds can grow through the soil you place and interfere with the crops you are growing. These can be removed by digging up the sod until only the ground is exposed. Alternatively, you can lay cardboard over the grass before placing your raised bed. The cardboard smothers the grass and weeds, and they eventually die. The cardboard will then later rot away, providing nutrients to the growing plants.

The location you choose to place your raised beds also needs to be easily protected from large pests. Rabbits, deer, raccoons, many types of birds, and rodents will find a veggie patch the ideal snacking grounds. Research what pests you have in your area and develop ways to protect your growing crop. It is important to remember some animals burrow while others can leap over inefficient fences.

Materials

What materials you need will depend on what kind of raised bed you want to build. The sides of a raised bed can be made with bricks, stacked stones (for mound beds), plastic wood, or even metal sheets. You can even splurge a little and buy raised bed kits, which are easier to construct than most homemade varieties. Many people find a 4 x 8-foot wooden raised bed aesthetically pleasing, while others prefer using concrete blocks. There are pros and cons for each, but at the end of the day, it comes down to what you can find or buy at a reasonable price.

When using wood, it is best to get those that come from cedar, black walnut, redwood, or oak. This wood is rot-resistant, giving you a longer-lasting raised bed. However, these types of wood are generally expensive and will drive up the cost of your raised bed. Consider using untreated pine to be more cost-effective. It may not last as many years, but it will last for several growing seasons before it starts to fall apart, adding to the organic material in the soil.

You can increase the longevity of the wood you use by treating it with linseed or tung oil—preferably the raw variety. The wood will need time to dry out after the application of the oil—roughly 10–30 minutes—before you can assemble the bed. Although you can use pressure-treated wood, it isn't advisable as you don't know what chemicals were used to treat the wood. These are the same chemicals that will leach out into the soil as soon as it is added. It is best to avoid this type of wood, or your crops may be affected.

The use of rocks or metal on the sides of a bed is great in the early and later parts of the growing season as they heat up better than wood. Unfortunately, this can also be a disadvantage at the height of summer, resulting in you having to water your beds more frequently to keep the plants cool.

Many people like to use cinder blocks—now more commonly known as cement blocks—to create their raised beds, but be careful of the composition of the blocks. The older cinder blocks used to be made with ash, some even with fly ash, which contained harmful chemicals that could leach into the soil. This is why it is important to only use solid blocks and not those that are broken. If unsure of the composition of the blocks that you are using, consider lining them.

Lining a raised bed isn't necessary, but if you want to prevent possible unknown chemicals from leaching out of wood or cement blocks, this will help. The best liner to use is BPA-free plastic (food-grade), such as the six-millimeter plastic sheeting usually used in creating hoop houses (mini-greenhouse attachment for raised beds). It is important that this plastic only lines the walls of your raised bed. You don't want to line the bottom as it will interfere with the drainage. When in an area where you have ground burrowing animals, such as groundhogs, consider adding a layer of rust-resistant wire mesh at the bottom of the bed. The holes in the mesh should be too small for the animal to burrow through but large enough to allow beneficial soil organisms through.

Troughs and metal drums make for beautiful raised beds. The main things to remember are that they need drainage holes and will require more water to prevent the soil from drying out. In addition, cooler-loving plants should be planted toward the center.

Spacing

Unlike a traditional veggie garden where you have to consider where to tread carefully, raised beds have walkways between them. Depending on the space available to you, you get to determine their size. This leaves the raised bed only for growing plants. Once you know the dimensions of your raised bed, you will need to consider how you will space the seedlings or seeds in it. Each plant has its own requirements. Some may need more room to spread out while others grow tall. Take this into consideration when you're planning where you will plant what.

Learn to use the growing plants to help each other. Plants that are just close enough to have their leaves touching, make for excellent shade within the bed, without shading out other plants. This foliage or cover shading helps to lower the temperature in the bed, prevents too much evaporation, and prevents insects from getting to the roots easily. Some leaves, such as cucumbers and some pumpkins, have prickles on them. This tactile irritation will prevent some animals from trying to get to your crops as they don't like to walk across them.

CREATING A RAISED BED

Most raised beds are made from wood or concrete blocks. Before buying any materials needed for this project, be sure to have a blueprint of what you want to build. Play around with designs to see which is more feasible space and pocket-wise.

Wooden

Raised beds made from wood don't last as long as those made from concrete blocks, but they look better and can be further decorated, which is a great project for children. Alternatively, you can write on the wood showing where certain seeds were planted in the bed. Using wood makes for a lighter raised bed that can be moved as a whole structure, if needed. The longevity of a wooden raised bed is only a couple of years. However, once it has served its purpose, it can be reused as organic matter in your compost heap.

A disadvantage of making a wooden raised bed is that you will need power tools to cut the wood down to size or to drill screws in place. If nervous about using power tools such as saws, have the planks cut at your closest local hardware store, or ask a friend for help.

The most common raised beds people like to build are 4 x 8 feet with a depth of 10 inches. However, this isn't a hard and fast rule. When using materials lying around, look at the lengths available to you. If you have 12-foot planks, consider a 3 x 6-foot bed instead. You want to cut as few times as possible and not have any waste remaining.

For the construction of a 4 x 8-foot with a depth of 10 inches, you will need roughly fifty-six 3-inch deck screws (rust-resistant), three 2 x 10 8-foot planks, and four 2 x 4 8-foot planks. You will also need a counter-sink drill bit and a table saw if you want to cut the planks to length yourself. It is important to pre-drill any holes you want to add screws to. Countersinking the holes allows for the screws to be flush with the side of the wood, preventing them from snagging on anything.

- Take one of the 2 x 10 planks and cut it in half. These will make up the width sections of the raised bed.
- Place an uncut 2 x 10 plank adjacent to the newly cut plank so that the shorter plank is on the inside to form an L-shape. Place the pieces

together so that the inside forms a 90°angle, and the edges of the plank are flush with each other.

- Pre-drill four holes along the height of the length plank into the width plank.
- When pre-drilling holes, ensure that you drill them roughly 0.75 inches from any edge as this will prevent the wood from splitting.
- Add the screws to pull the two pieces together to form the first corner. Repeat this with the other planks and corners until you have the rectangular bed shape.
- For added strength and a place to sit along the edges of the bed, you will add the 2 x 4 planks.
- Start by taking one of the 2 x 4 planks and cut it into eight 1-inch sections. These will be the cleats used to add extra support to the railing.
- Add two cleats to the inside of each wall. They will need to be level with the top of each side. For the longer sides, add a cleat a third of the length down, and another a further third down. For the shorter sides, add to the corners created.
- Use two screws per cleat, aim to have them diagonal to each other for best stability.
- Once all the cleats are in place, place the first railing along with one of the longer lengths of

the bed. Add the screws from one end to the other to prevent the wood from bowing.

- You will need to drill eight holes (in groups of two) along the length of the railing. Start with two at the first end, then move to the first cleat. You will need to drill one hole in the cleat and another in the railing. With a hole in the cleat and the length edge, when the railing is added, it allows for extra support. Try to space the screws by two inches diagonally from each other.
- Repeat for the next cleat before pre-drilling the last holes at the end of the length.
- Add the screws from one end to the other. Repeat for the final long side.
- Using the last 2 x 4 plank, measure the width between the two length railings and cut to size.
- Follow the same drilling practice for the width, ensuring that one screw is in the cleat and the other is in the width edge. Repeat for both cleats on both sides.
- Ensure the raised bed is level before filling it with your preferred soil combination.

If you want a sturdier wooden raised bed, especially if you are planning a bed deeper than 10 inches, consider adding a post to each of the corners. By screwing the planks directly to the post, you offer more strength to your overall raised bed, allowing it to contain more soil. You can even partially bury these posts to ensure the raised bed isn't easily tipped over.

Concrete Blocks

If you can find concrete blocks with a central hole, these are generally the best to use. This extra space on the outside of the raised bed is perfect to plant flowers and herbs which need to be controlled. These plants can act as companion plants that attract beneficial insects while deterring harmful ones.

Depending on the size and shape of the blocks available to you, they can be fairly affordable, plus you don't need to buy many. Although how many you need will be dependent on the size and shape of the bed you want to make.

The advantage of using concrete blocks is that you don't need any power tools, nor do you need to measure and cut anything, the blocks easily fit next to each other. The bed can easily be disassembled when moving and doesn't rot away. The disadvantage is that they are heavy, and you will need gloves to work with them to prevent you from getting hurt while handling them.

Concrete blocks come in many sizes and thicknesses. Aim to use blocks measuring roughly a foot in length and 10 inches in height, as these will be the easiest to use when making a raised bed. Again, this isn't a set rule, and you can use what is available to you. However, ensure the blocks are whole to make building and lining up easier. Calculate how many blocks of a certain size you will need to make the desired size raised bed.

- Ensure the area you are using is completely flat. To help the blocks settle well, put them on a flat surface such as grass (which will be smothered), dirt, or on cardboard.
- Lay out the number of blocks needed to get the desired shape and size you want. Ensure they are sitting tightly against each other to prevent gaps in which soil can fall through.
- Place the blocks so that the central hole is pointing upward.
- Edges should line up to create a 90° angle inside the bed when building a square or rectangular shape.
- The blocks shouldn't fall over. Stabilize the blocks well by adding soil to the central hole.
- Fill up until an inch from the top of the bed with the preferred organic matter and soil.

- If you want a deeper bed, add a secondary layer of blocks over the first.

Unlike wooden raised beds, you can leave a small section open while you are filling the bed with soil. That way you can bring a wheelbarrow into the bed to drop off the soil. Once you get to a point where you are running out of space for the wheelbarrow, you can remove it, close the wall, then continue to fill the bed until satisfied with the depth.

Don't place plants in every central hole of the blocks. This will impede your ability to sit and reach toward the middle of the bed. You can even use the holes along one edge of the raised bed to make a trellis that can be used to coax plants to grow vertically.

CROP ROTATION

Some people believe crop rotation isn't necessary for a raised bed garden, while others would disagree. Crop rotation is a sure way to keep the soil you are growing in healthy no matter what you try to grow.

Why Rotate Crops?

As plants grow, they consume minerals and other nutrients in the soil. Some plants are heavier feeders and will drain the soil more readily than lighter feeders or givers (plants that return nitrogen to the soil). By growing the same types of plants over and over, many minerals aren't returned to the soil. By not replacing these minerals, it can lead to a deficiency in the soil. Plants grown in deficient soils fail to thrive, as they don't have what they need to develop properly.

Some plants release chemicals into the soil that can affect the growth of other plants (allelopathy). These chemicals can be damaging. By planting similar plants year in and year out, the ground can become a hotbed of diseases and insects that prey on that particular group. Plants constantly attacked by diseases and pests don't grow well and will have lower yields.

By rotating different types of plants over the years, the soil remains healthy and pest free. This results in good growth and high yields every year. However, crop rotation can be tricky, reiterating why you should plan where you want to plant every season. By keeping track, you will prevent overlapping of similar groups of plants being planted in the same locations, time and time again.

You can even help crops from the plant you grow next growth season with what you plant now. Potatoes have an extensive root system, and you're required to dig up the crops to get to them. This loosened soil is now perfect for planting carrots. Crop rotation is all about working toward the future health of your raised bed.

How to Rotate Crops

The most important part of crop rotation is understanding that plants, especially vegetables, are divided into specific groups. You need to identify these groups to ensure you don't grow plants from the same group yearly in the same place. There are seven main groups of vegetables:

- Alliums, the onion family (e.g. onions, shallots, and garlic)
- legumes (peas and beans)
- Brassicas, the mustard and cabbage family (e.g. broccoli, cauliflowers, cabbage, and radishes)
- Solanaceae, the nightshade family (e.g. peppers, potatoes, and tomatoes)
- Umbelliferae, the carrot family (e.g. carrots, dill, and parsnips)
- cucurbits, the squash family (e.g. pumpkins, cucumbers, and squashes)
- Chenopodiaceae, the beet family (e.g. chard, beet greens, beets, and spinach)

Other vegetables, such as lettuce, don't fall into these groups. Lettuce can be planted whenever with or after these families without any problems. This is similarly true for flowers and herbs.

Take the list of plants you want to grow and see which groups they fall into. Once you know what group they fall into, you know what you can plant the following year. The general rule is that you shouldn't plant the same group within the same space within a 3–5 year cycle—although this can be dependent from plant to plant. This is not to say the entire bed cannot have a particular crop in it the following year; it just means you can't grow in the same place within the bed as the previous year.

Map out your raised bed on paper for the next few years to see which crop rotation is best for you, so you can enjoy all the plants you want to grow. Color code each group of plants and make your raised bed maps colorful. Keep these handy when you start planting so that you remember what your plan was. Alternatively, you can use online garden planners, which take the guesswork out of what plants belong in which groups. Some programs can store previous planting plans and warn you if you are planting the wrong group in the wrong section of your raised bed.

Using some of the vegetables already discussed in the earlier chapter, let's build a crop rotation system that is easy to understand:

- Legumes and alliums like rich soil and benefit from a freshly fertilized raised bed. Legumes also produce extra nitrogen in the soil, which benefits anything that grows after it.
- Nitrogen-rich soil is best for heavy nitrogen feeders from the brassica group. Radishes are best planted in the same spot after legumes.
- The following season this piece of the raised bed is perfect for some plants from the Solanaceae group. Plant as many tomatoes or potatoes as allowed in this section.
- Once the Solanaceae plants are dug up, the ground is nice and soft, perfect for the development of carrots from the Umbelliferae group.
- After this, you can decide if you want to grow anything from the cucurbit group (cucumbers) or the Chenopodiaceae group (chard).

The easiest way to understand crop rotation is to not plant the same groups of plants in the same spot every growing season. It's all about the advantages each of the different groups can give you during the current and following season.

As important as what crop rotation is between the different types of vegetables you plant, also consider how well different groups of plants may help each other. A perfect example of how plants support each other is seen in the Native American planting strategy known as the Three Sisters.

Before there were man-made items such as pesticides and shade cloth readily available, people of the past had to figure out ways to get the best from their crops with what they had. This was where the Three Sister planting strategy came from, and it is something you can still plant in your own raised bed to get the best of three very different plants.

By combining sweet corn, climbing beans, and squash, you can get several benefits to your raised bed. The sweet corn acts as a support for the climbing beans to grow vertically. The beans fix nitrogen to the soil, which acts as a fertilizer for the corn and the squash. The squash grows around the beans and corn, adding extra shade, increasing water retention, as well as warding off pesky raccoons, which find their leaves too prickly to walk across to reach the growing crops.

BEST PLANTS FOR A RAISED BED

Most of the plants discussed in Chapter 1 are perfect for raised bed gardening, as long as you take into consideration their individual needs in space and other requirements. Depending on the depth of the raised bed you constructed, you can grow just about anything in it, and are not limited to only vegetables. Here are a few more examples of great additions to your raised bed.

Onions

Onions can be grown from seed but can be tricky to germinate if the conditions aren't ideal. Most people either germinate them indoors or plant an onion set (bulb). You must know the correct way to plant the set, or the plant will struggle to grow. The rounded part of the set needs to go into the ground, while the more pointed part needs to point to the top. Onions are a fine example of what you see above ground is what you see below; they need space to grow. You can enjoy the leaves in salads, or wait till they turn yellow and fall over, as this will let you know that the onion is ready to be dug up.

Garlic

Similar to onions, garlic is best grown from sets. However, don't assume store-bought garlic will give the same results as sets sold from garden centers. By getting sets from the garden center, you are sure of what variety you are growing and what to expect from its growth. Garlic takes a long time to grow (7–8 months, if not more). The hardiness zone you plant in will have a large effect on your ability to grow this vegetable.

Peas

Peas are similar to beans as they come in bush and trellis varieties. Not only that but some varieties are best eaten shelled, while others have edible pods. Peas can be grown from seeds, but depending on the variety, the seeds may need to be soaked for a few hours before planting. The planted seeds need to be protected from rodents as they make for a protein-packed meal.

Arugula

Arugula, also known as rocket, is the more flavorful cousin of the lettuce. Its peppery taste is well received in salads and even on burgers to give a unique taste. This plant requires rich soil and plenty of sunshine to thrive. Leaves are prone to wilting if you don't keep up with their water needs. The younger the leaves, the tastier they are raw, while the older leaves retain more of their peppery flavor when cooked.

Patty Pans

Patty pans—also known as custard marrows—are wonderfully flavorful squashes that come in a variety of colors, shapes, and sizes. This squash can have its skin eaten, whereas others are less palatable or too thick to consume. As with other squashes, if allowed to grow unrestricted, it will soon take over the bed. It is a good idea to encourage this plant to grow vertically to save on space. Patty pans are best grown from seeds—up to three in a hole—and later thinned out to prevent competition. They love growing in full sunshine and will need a lot of water to help bulk their crop size.

Spinach

Growing spinach is almost as quick as lettuce and just as tasty as there are many different varieties available on the market. This vegetable can be enjoyed straight off the plant or cooked and is a great way to get some extra plant-based iron into your diet. The best way to grow spinach is stagger planting, allowing you to produce tasty leaves throughout the growing season.

Beetroot (Beets)

Beetroot is a very versatile vegetable. The smaller and younger you dig the crop up, the sweeter the bulbs will be, making them perfect raw in a salad, or boil and serve them as a hot vegetable. However, if you allow them to grow too long, the bulb can become woody and tough. Thankfully, the vegetable won't be wasted if this happens, as it can be pickled to get rid of its toughness. Beets, like radishes, will only produce a single crop per seed. Staggering the growth of beets throughout a growing season will give you a nearly endless supply of fresh crops. Don't ignore the greens of beets! They taste similar to chard, and if you take the outer leaves from the plant now and again, you prevent the plant from overcrowding and overshadowing its neighbor. It is best planted from seed as it is a root crop.

Don't feel limited by this list, as many herbs and flowers go well in a raised bed. Consider adding plants such as basil or marigolds to help guard against pesky insects while attracting beneficial insects that pollinate your flowers or act as predators of pest species. When using a wooden raised bed, these plants can be added in rows or containers around the bed. With a concrete block raised bed, these plants can be added around the perimeter in the central holes in the blocks.

3

UP, UP, AND AWAY! VERTICAL GARDENING

S pace is in high demand. Consider how much land is available in a city, and you will quickly understand why skyscrapers exist. By concentrating on building vertically up, a small piece of land can generate far more than just using it horizontally. This is the premise of vertical gardening.

With a small piece of land, or even just a wall or fence, you can create a hanging garden that produces a variety of plants. Growing vertically is as easy as rummaging in your garage to upcycle something or as complicated as what you can build.

The main thing is to understand what plants you want to grow and what they need. Some plants need deep roots and can't be added to something like a pocket

planter. While other plants may be of the vining variety, which needs support and do well with growing along a trellis. Whatever you decide to use, just remember that you are growing up and not sideways.

ADVANTAGES AND DISADVANTAGES

The main benefit to vertical gardening is that you don't need much space. In addition, you may already have the necessary vertical supports available around your home. By growing vertically, you can harvest more easily. There is less bending and squatting to pick your crop if it is growing at eye level. There is some initial ground-level work that needs to be done, but once you have coaxed the plants to grow up a trellis—especially when combined with a raised bed—you can enjoy watching the plants grow high. However, when growing vertically, don't allow the structures you create to be taller than what you can reach to harvest and care for what you grow.

When deciding to grow vertically, consider how you want to do this and if you want to combine it with your already established garden or raised bed. Most trellises will need to be added to raised beds before planting seeds or transplants to prevent any damage to them.

By growing vertically, your plants greatly benefit from the little space they originally started in. There is less chance of disease and pests from the ground affecting the plant as less of it is in contact with the dirt. Diseases and pests are more readily noticed and can be dealt with accordingly in a vertical garden. Watering strategies allow you to water exactly where you need to, preventing overwatering or getting the foliage excessively wet. There is more airflow through a vertical garden, leading to fewer fungal infections affecting your plants. More of the leaves are exposed to the sun, meaning the plant grows better and produces more crops. With the plant not sprawled out on the ground, there is less chance of you accidentally damaging it— knocking immature fruit or blossoms off—as you care for it. With less ground to look after, there will be fewer weeds you need to concern yourself with.

As a bonus factor, you can create living walls that not only produce delicacies but block unsavory sights or nosy neighbors and create a windbreak. A trellis can also be used to create shade to help produce crops at the height of summer when they prefer cooler temperatures.

Depending on what kind of vertical gardening you are trying, there may be some disadvantages when it comes to watering and getting the required sunlight. Vertical gardens backed by a wall or fence may find themselves in a rain shadow, where the structure prevents the water from landing on the plants. Vertical gardens greatly benefit from drip irrigation on a timer. The type of container you use for vertical gardening will influence how often you should water or even fertilize. The size and depth of the container will also be a constraint on what you can and can't grow.

WHAT TO USE TO GROW VERTICALLY

You're only limited by your imagination. Whether you buy kits, upcycle, or purchase items to make a vertical garden, it is completely up to you and what you can afford or repurpose.

Upcycling

When using upcycled materials to grow in, be sure to use products that are food-grade, especially when it comes to plastic or metal. Also, consider what the plant needs in terms of space to grow. Some plants such as chives, microgreens, and some varieties of lettuce only need 3–4 inches of soil, while plants such as garlic, peppers, cabbage, and peas will need 5–8 inches. Any container you plan to use needs to be deep enough to grow what you want. Plants that require 8–15 inches for their roots are best planted in pots or a raised bed with possibly needing a vertical trellis system. This will include woody herbs such as mint, large squashes, and daikon radishes. Know what can be planted in a container versus your raised bed.

Once you have decided what you want to plant, look around in your garage, yard sales, or Goodwill for any containers which would be ideal for vertical planters. Wooden boxes on brackets attached in a staggered pattern on a vertical pole can make for a beautiful centerpiece in your garden. Alternatively, the brackets can be attached to the posts on your porch to get the same effect. The brackets are important as they offer extra support to the boxes as they get quite heavy with moistened soil and any plants you grow.

Old baskets, woven or made of metal, can be added to walls or fences and filled with any plant you want. Metal baskets may need to be lined with a fine mesh to prevent the soil from falling through while still allowing excess water to drain. Baskets are generally cheap and can be found anywhere. Ensure they are tightly connected to whatever vertical source you add them to. Add some brackets for extra support, if needed.

Old gutters and PVC pipes can be hung from railings in a ladder-like fashion. As long as they have the necessary drainage holes in place, you can grow your microgreens on your back porch. Never again do you need to take more than a couple of steps to get fresh produce ready for your salad.

Old wooden pallets have many uses! They can be broken down and used in the construction of a raised bed, or they can be used as a vertical garden bed. Take some landscaping fabric and staple it in place along the back and sides. Make individual pockets per horizontal section to have 3–4 horizontal planters—depending on the design and size of the pallet. It is important to ensure the pallet is stable against a surface so that it can't be tipped over by the wind. Fill the pockets with potting soil and seeds or transplants, then water and watch them grow.

You can even create a vertical garden in your house. Collect a few food-grade cans and place them on several shelves in the kitchen. With some drainage holes—and something to catch the leaks—you can have fresh oregano, parsley, and basil growing in your kitchen. Ready at any time to be added to a bubbling pot of soup or stew. These cans can also bring color to your kitchen when you paint them.

If those ideas aren't enough to tickle your creativity, consider using old milk jugs, large soda bottles, or fruit juice bottles to make a hanging vertical garden. You will need several bottles with their lids and some garden twine to make this unique vertical planter:

- Lay the bottles on their sides and cut a portion from the top of the bottle. It is important to retain most of the sides and some of the top because it helps with the stability and integrity of the bottle.

- Add four holes at the two ends of the bottle; two at the top and two at the bottom. You will be adding the garden twine through these sections.
- Prepare several bottles like this.
- Thread enough of the garden twine through the holes to have each bottle separated by 1–1.5 feet.
- To prevent the bottles from sliding down, add a knot under each hole to keep it from moving.
- Keep the bottles as level as possible.
- Attach the garden twine well to a wall or balcony.
- Fill with potting soil and water then add transplants or seeds.
- Enjoy as the plants start to grow.

What you can grow in this vertical planter will be affected by the shape and volume of the bottle. You can also use this idea to connect several lengths of gutters or PVC piping. These are only some of the ideas you can use when upcycling items. Look at what is available to you and come up with your own ideas. Be wary of the weight you add to the garden twine. It can only carry so much. Consider doubling up on twine, or some thin paracord, for extra support.

Purchasing

Vertical planter pots are ideal for growing multiple herbs and microgreens and can be placed anywhere in your garden or on a balcony. Deep pots allow you to grow plants that have deeper root systems. However, they can be rather expensive, despite being beautiful.

Planter boxes with built-in trellises allow you to grow cucurbits easily without needing much space and a piece of ground in the garden. They are perfect for growing a full salad on your balcony or porch. Alternatively, pocket planters can be attached to walls and fences before being filled with potting soil and plants. These are perfect for smaller herbs and microgreens. Depending on the number of pockets available, you are spoiled for choice when it comes to filling them.

Trellises and Supports

Vertical growing can be combined with an existing raised bed in terms of supports or trellises for plants that are rambling, sprawling, or a climbing variety. When deciding on the support you want to use, you need to consider the material you will use to make it, the elements it will be exposed to, and how easy it is to maintain.

Generally, supports are found inside a raised bed, while trellises are along the edges. It comes down to the design you want to incorporate into the look of your garden. Most trellises can be bought from garden centers. However, if you are creative and have the time, you can use several materials to make supports and trellises.

Simple bamboo canes or stakes can be planted next to a seedling, which is then tied to it—as seen with tomatoes tied to stakes. Using poles is a great way to encourage growth within a row. When planting several poles, it is a good idea to have horizontal support tied to the top to add to the strength of the structure. Several horizontal poles can also be tied in place to help plants with larger crops (squashes) from pulling the whole structure down. By doing this, you also increase the growing area that the plant has access to.

If you aren't overly concerned with planting in rows, you can consider a teepee or wigwam for plants such as peas and beans. You will need about eight poles arranged equally in a circular shape. Tie the upper ends about a foot from the top to stabilize the poles together. You can wedge this structure down into the ground to prevent it from blowing over. Around the legs of the teepee shape, you can plant your seeds. Once sprouted, they can be coaxed to grow upwards. You can either have the plant naturally wrap around the poles or help it a little by tying it in place. Don't tie it too tightly, as the plant will continue to grow and may be cut off from its roots if the ties are too tight.

When growing plants with large crops, bamboo won't cut it, and you will need sturdier support. You can turn to sawn-off branches of trees or elaborate trellises made of wood or metal. The heavier and more abundant the crop produced by the plants, the sturdier your support structure will need to be. When using trellises, they must be stabilized as much as possible. This will result in the trellis being secured to a wall or posts.

Perhaps you don't want to limit yourself to a standard wall trellis. If this is the case, why not consider an archway trellis? This type of trellis is stunning to look at, and when spun over a walkway between raised beds, it utilizes the space of the walkway without you stepping on your plants. These types of trellises can be purchased premade, or you can construct them yourself using wood or cattle or livestock fencing.

To use fencing, you will likely need roughly 16 feet of fencing to get the perfect arch that has a width of 6 feet and a top that is easily reached. This is no easy project to do by yourself, so ensure that there is someone who can help you with getting the necessary materials and can help bend the fencing into shape.

For an archway made of cattle fencing, you will need about 16 feet of 4-gauge fencing—this can be one whole section or several smaller sections—and either eight 3-foot posts or eight 9.5-inch landscape stakes. It may also be a good idea to handle the fencing with gloves.

- Between two people—or you and a wall—shape the arch by bringing one end toward the other while the fencing lies on its side.

- Once the arch is shaped to the dimensions you want—size-dependent—then set it upright and place it over the raised bed of choice.
- Hammer four stakes into the ground at regular intervals per side of the fencing.
- Alternatively, hammer in the posts and tie the fence to it securely.

The best way to position the arch is along the edge of one bed and then over the walkway and its neighbor. This will result in one of the beds being in the shade during some part of the day. This makes the bed perfect for cooler temperature-loving plants, such as carrots, lettuce, and broccoli.

Archways make for beautiful additions to the garden but can be semi-permanent. Before adding one to your raised beds, add it to your plan on paper to see if it is feasible and if you have the space for it.

BEST PLANTS FOR VERTICAL GARDENS

Most plants can be grown vertically if you have the correct container and support. The best way to see what works in your garden is to experiment with what vertical garden you have designed.

Non-Trellis

When planting a non-trellised vertical garden, you need to consider the root systems of the plants you want to grow. Shallow roots, as seen in radishes, chives, green and spring onions, Parisian carrots, microgreens, and leaf lettuce, only need about four inches of soil to grow comfortably in.

For larger root systems, such as watermelon radishes, cabbage, baby beets, and bush varieties of beans and peas, you will need a minimum of 5–8 inches of soil. When planting large plants, such as pumpkins, daikon radishes, mints, and summer squashes, you will need at least 15 inches of soil. These plants may also need some sort of support to help them grow as the season progresses.

Trellis

Any plant that would sprawl is perfect for growing vertically. However, the size of the crop needs to be taken into consideration before selecting the type of support you will need. While the teepee support structure with bamboo is perfect for most bean or pea varieties, it isn't appropriate for squashes of any kind.

The plants that do well in a trellised vertical garden are beans, peas, tomatoes, cucumbers, squash, and melons (if you are interested in growing some fruit). While beans and peas are generally lightweight, the others are fairly heavy and may need some extra support.

When growing vegetables such as pumpkins and summer squashes, some varieties have large fruits you need to be aware of. The higher up this fruit develops, the more strain is placed on the stem connecting the fruit to the plant. To prevent these fruit from falling from the trellis support, you will need to consider how you will protect them.

Something as simple as a nylon stocking split open and cut in half can be used as a hammock to support a single squash weighing 2–3 pounds. By tying the stocking to the trellis and placing the squash within the hammock can drastically reduce the strain on the stem. Nylon stockings aren't the only way to support large fruiting vegetables. Socks are great for smaller fruits, while hammocks can be fashioned from any material to help carry the weight. You can even hang containers to hold the vegetables. However, be sure to have drainage holes ready if it rains, and be aware that when a growing fruit is constrained, it will take on the shape it is forced into.

Tomatoes can grow multiple feet in length, depending on the variety. Be prepared to cut the points of the growing stem to stop their vertical growth. The plant uses a lot of energy to grow vertically, and will often prevent itself from developing blossoms if it is putting too much effort into growing. By limiting the vertical growth, you can encourage that energy to go into preparing blossoms and ripening fruit.

Experiment with different trellises and vertical gardens to see which best suits the plants you want to grow in your small garden or even indoors.

4

A LITTLE SPACE CAN CREATE A HUGE BOUNTY! CONTAINER GARDENING 101

With containers, you are no longer limited to growing outside, but rather have a plant that can be moved to where you believe it will do best. Container gardening is exactly what it says: gardening in a container. What that container is, it doesn't matter! As long as it can hold soil and a plant it is worthy of gardening in.

ADVANTAGES AND DISADVANTAGES

This is the perfect way to garden if you have no space outside, yet you have an area on your balcony, patio, or even inside your home that gets enough sunshine to grow your preferred vegetables. The best part of container gardens? They can go with you wherever you decide to go, unlike raised beds or constructed vertical gardens. If you have a perennial plant—a plant that lasts longer than one growing season—that you want to protect from the frost, it is as simple as bringing it indoors. Plus, you can grow a special plant for that special someone as a gift.

Container gardening lowers water waste as when you water you are directly watering into the container and nowhere else. You will have fewer pests as the soil you are using won't have any creepy crawlies hiding in it. You can also monitor what is happening in the container more readily than out in a larger raised bed. When you notice problems such as fungal growth, you can move the containers to lower the humidity and treat the affected plants easier. You are in control of every aspect of a container and, therefore, the growing conditions of the plants in them. Move them when you need more sun, or bring them inside when there are warnings of black frost or major storms.

Containers are more convenient than other forms of gardening. They are always on hand for when you want the freshest produce. Just reach out and pick what you need. It is also the easiest way to get children interested in gardening. It isn't as labor-intensive as a raised bed, and with smaller containers, even the youngest of toddlers can move them with ease to the right spot.

HOW TO MAKE A CONTAINER GARDEN FROM SCRATCH

Container gardening is so easy that anyone can do it. However, to get a successful garden with this planting strategy, you must follow guidelines to ensure the health of the plants you want to grow.

Size Does Matter

When it comes to gardening in containers, it is all about size. Too small and the plant suffers; too large and you suffer trying to move it around. Small-sized containers don't allow plants to reach their mature size, and you will be forced to pot them out to larger containers. Smaller containers also don't hold a lot of water and will require frequent watering, which can lead to other problems farther down the line. Although a larger container seems like a great idea, remember that you may have to move it at some point. If an empty container is too heavy for you to move, don't even consider it! Once it has damp soil and a fruiting plant in it, it will be impossible to carry.

When considering the right size of the container, think of the depth the roots need to grow. A container that is too shallow will dry out too quickly. The plant won't get enough water and nutrients to support itself, and the plant won't have a deep enough root system to support its height. By having the right depth, the soil can retain moisture for longer, lowering the number of times you need to water the container. Many people believe a 5-gallon container is best for growing vegetables, but this is up to your discretion and what you want to plant. However, anything with a depth of 12 inches is enough for most plants you want to grow, with some needing more or less.

Container Types

The container type will also play a heavy role in its weight. Glazed and unglazed (terracotta) ceramics are beautiful additions to a container garden. They come in various shapes and sizes, and glazed ceramics tend to be more durable than unglazed varieties. However, they are heavy and expensive, and when dropped, they will shatter. Not only that, but during colder winters, they may crack, making them useless to you. Ceramics generally need to be emptied and stored away during winter when outside, defeating the purpose of having a container you can use throughout the year.

Plastic containers are inexpensive, come in a variety of colors, shapes, and sizes, and are light enough to move around with ease. However, they need to be food-grade to prevent chemicals from leaching into the soil while the plants grow. The color you choose is also vital as lighter colors absorb less heat while darker colors absorb more. Take your local temperature into consideration when choosing the color of your containers.

You can even consider using wooden containers. As long as the wood hasn't been treated, you are spoiled for choice in size and shape. You can even make your own if you have the tools and a design in mind. The downside of wooden containers is that they don't last long, and after several years, they will start to rot. Another disadvantage is that a wooden container may be heavier than anticipated once constructed.

Fabric pots are another container you can consider. They are light, washable, breathable, reusable, and come with handles, making them easier to move around. The material allows water and air to move through it freely, leading to healthier roots. However, this also allows the soil to dry out easier, so it will need more frequent watering.

Best Soil for Your Container

Garden soil may be readily available, but it is a big no-no! Garden soil tends to compact too tightly and can carry a host of bacteria, viruses, and pests that can cause havoc on your container garden. Once in a container, this is where your plant will remain, and if it doesn't have the nutrients it needs, it won't thrive. Everything your plant needs has to be in the container.

Preferably you want to use potting soil in your container, and not just any potting soil, but a brand that states it is for growth in containers. You don't even need to buy this if you know how to mix up your own potting soil. A combination of compost (nutrients), vermiculite or perlite (water retention), and peat (soil structure) is all your plant needs to grow at its optimum. Adding granulated fertilizer to the potting soil is a must if it isn't added already. The plant will need the extra nutrients as repetitive watering can cause the nutrients to be flushed away.

Whatever potting mix you decide to use, the mixture must be light and well aerated. This will allow the plant's root system to grow unabated and allow water to drain well. Just a tip, fill the pots in roughly the same area where you want them to stand. There is nothing worse than having to carry a heavy pot to its intended location once you have filled it.

Fertilize Those Babies

Plants don't have the same freedom in a container as they would in a raised bed. Instead of forcing the roots to seek out the necessary nutrients, give them exactly what they need when needed. Although fertilizer is premixed into the potting soil before you add the plant, this isn't enough. Container gardens need to be watered more than other gardens, resulting in more nutrients and minerals being washed away. These will need to be replaced.

Many people believe that adding some slow-releasing fertilizer granules to the top of the container is enough. Each subsequent watering breaks down the granules, releasing the nutrients and minerals the plants need to thrive. However, this isn't your only option. Liquid formulations—such as manure tea or emulsified fish— can be added every two weeks after the plant is a few weeks old to help with the diet it needs to grow health-ily. Alternatively, you can put your compost to work as mulch. By spreading a layer of compost at the top of the container, you provide the protection that mulch gives, and as you water, the nutrients from it are leached out into the soil.

Following the Sun

As with all gardens, the location is vital to the growth of your plants. Most vegetables need a minimum of six hours, but herbs and microgreens require a little less. Finding a sunny spot on a balcony or in your home can be a little more tricky than out in the garden, but it is possible. From the time the sun rises to the time it sets, keep an eye out for sunny spots that appear. Once you note a sunny spot, see how long it appears in that particular area. Keep checking it at intervals of 30 minutes. If the spot receives more than six hours of sunlight, it is the perfect spot for your containers.

However, in taller buildings in cities, you may find you don't get enough sun all the time. No worries! A few grow lights strategically placed will allow your small container garden to flourish. As the seasons change and the location of the sunlight starts to alter, you can move your containers to ensure they get the sun they require.

When lucky enough to have some space outside, think of how you can best utilize the space that you have available to you. A series of bricks and planks—or even stairs—give rise to a vertical container garden. By doing this, you can have taller plants in the back that can be supported by a trellis, while in the front, you can have your shorter plants. Remember to place the plants in such a way that they all receive the sunlight they need.

Too much sun can also be bad as it dries the containers out too quickly. Use the naturally occurring shade of taller plants to help with the shading of plants that prefer cooler temperatures.

Container gardens need to be guarded against the wind. The wind can sap the moisture from plants or cause them to topple. Containers with particularly large plants are prone to catching the wind and toppling, especially if the container isn't particularly heavy. This can damage the containers, the falling plant, and other plants and containers when it falls down on them. A windbreak made of shade cloth or heavier containers with tall plants can help protect lighter and smaller containers from being toppled.

By clustering several containers together, you can create a microclimate that is different from the local climate. This can both be an advantage and a disadvantage. In a microclimate, the many plants together can create an environment with higher humidity. This will lower the need to water as frequently but will also increase the chance of fungal infections spreading from plant to plant. You will need to be a little more vigilant with your container gardens than any other kind of garden.

Temperature is crucial for the germination of seeds. If the soil is below 60 °F most seeds will struggle to germinate, while some seedlings will struggle to thrive. When germinating plants inside, take the time to get them accustomed to going outside a few hours a day. Don't assume they will be fine if there is a cold snap during the evening. Harden all indoor seedlings to make the move to the outside.

When choosing a location for your containers, you need to consider the area's weight tolerance. Over-crowding a balcony with large containers can affect its structural integrity. When moving containers, the best exposure to sunlight will come from the west and south in the northern hemisphere, while in the southern hemisphere, it's the opposite. Unless you have an automatic watering system, have your containers close to a source of water. Otherwise, you will be carrying water back and forth for hours every day, taking away from the joy of gardening.

Watering and Drainage Is Key

Container gardens tend to dry out quickly due to many reasons (sun, wind, size, etc.), so coming up with a watering strategy that works for you is key. Containers need to be kept moist but not overwatered as this will leach out all the important nutrients and minerals the plants need. It is a fine line you will need to walk to ensure the health of your plants. Luckily, there are several strategies you can use.

The first is to purchase self-watering containers. These containers vary in size and come with a reservoir you can fill with water which then seeps up through the soil to keep the roots moist. The larger these containers, the more likely they will be on wheels, making your life significantly easier as they get very heavy. You must check the water volume in the reservoir now and again, especially as the plant grows and its need for water increases. Be warned that these containers can come with a hefty price tag the larger they are.

You can also construct your own drip irrigation—there are many DIY videos on the internet—that are attached to a timer to water your plants. Alternatively, lift the containers—if possible—once they are filled with moist soil. The weight will decrease as the soil starts to dry out. Although this is a good indication of moisture level, it isn't something everyone can do. Your best option will be to do the finger test.

Push your finger into the soil about an inch to see if there is any moisture in the top inch of the container. If there isn't, it is time to water your container. Some containers may need water up to twice a day depending on size and the environmental conditions. However, you mustn't just water the container because it is there, regardless of size. Too much water is as bad as too little, which brings us to drainage.

Drainage in a container is vital, especially if too much water is accidentally added—which is more of a common occurrence than people think. The excess water needs to go somewhere. All containers you use to grow plants need to either have a large central hole or several smaller drainage holes throughout the bottom. If the excess water has nowhere to go—and you keep adding more—it will remain standing at the bottom of the container, eventually going stagnant and anaerobic. Once this happens, your plant can potentially be exposed to bacteria, which could affect its growth at best or kill it at worst.

Where you place containers can affect whether they can drain or not. If the bottom of the container is flush with the surface it is on, there is a chance that the drainage holes become sealed and don't drain appropriately. This can be avoided by using containers that have a slight ridge around the bottom of it or by adding the container on pot feet. The containers will need to be elevated slightly to encourage healthy drainage. Remember to add a tray under any containers that are indoors, or the excess water may leak out onto your floors and carpets.

When creating drainage holes, be mindful of the sizes that you make. Too large and the soil can fall through it, too small and the container won't drain well. Rather have several 0.25–0.5-inch holes than one large one when you make drainage holes. To prevent soil from leaking out these holes, you can add some small pebbles before adding soil or even use a coffee filter to hold it back.

BEST VEGETABLES TO GROW IN CONTAINERS

Once more, what you grow will depend on the size of the container you are using. Plants from the Solanaceae group (tomato, peppers, etc.) do well when planted in containers.

Eggplants

Eggplants are also part of the Solanaceae group and enjoyed by many in all sorts of dishes. This unique vegetable comes in a variety of shapes, stunning colors, and patterns. This plant is best grown during the warmer parts of the year as it is sensitive to the cold—anything below 50 °F—and will be killed by a late frost.

Potatoes

Many people assume potatoes require too much space to grow in a container, but they'd be wrong. It all comes down to the size of the container and the type you use. Potato sacks are perfect for growing potatoes, but you will need at least a depth of 24 inches—depending on variety—to contain the growing spuds below the ground. You will also need to practice hilling to ensure your potatoes don't go green. As potatoes grow below the surface of the ground, some will breach the surface, and as soon as they spend some time in the sun, they will start to go green. Green potatoes produce a toxic alkaloid known as solanine, which causes several gastrointestinal issues when consumed. To prevent this, soil needs to be added to where the potatoes surface, generally close to the stem. Potatoes can take up to three months to grow to maturity. Consider which varieties you want to grow to lower the waiting time and the container size you will use.

Other plants which benefit from growing in containers include a wide range of salad greens (head forming or loose leaves), radishes of all kinds, cucumbers, carrots, spinach, onions, garlic, and small-to-medium summer squashes. You will have to avoid the larger pumpkins as the plant and the fruit will take up too much space in the container and your home! Brassicas such as cauliflower and broccoli are perfect for container growth.

Broccoli

Broccoli is a cool temperature-loving plant that is high in minerals and vitamins. The higher the temperature, the more of the head development is affected. You can grow the head to the size you prefer before picking it after it matures. However, as soon as the leaves start turning yellow, you must harvest the head as the quality starts to diminish after this stage. Both the head and the leaves—which resemble and taste like cabbage leaves—are edible. There are many varieties, some of which are heat tolerant, while others are great for freezing, allowing you to grow a large crop and then store it during winter.

Bush forms of peas and beans are preferable, but with the right trellis system, you can grow the climbing variety if you have a place for it. Unfortunately, plants such as corn don't do well in containers as they grow too tall and will topple too easily. You can also look at varieties of vegetables that are dwarf or container varieties, as these will also thrive in containers. Seed packets and even seed catalogs will have information about how high a plant will grow.

GROWING INDOORS

The best aspect of container gardens is that you aren't limited to growing outside. As soon as the weather turns nasty, bring your containers inside and continue to harvest crops throughout the colder months.

To have a successful container garden indoors, you need to follow all the parameters set for container gardens: location, container type and size, drainage, watering strategy, soil, and fertilizer. As long as you are realistic about the space inside your home, you can grow anything inside it.

The main problem with growing inside is that there isn't always an ideal spot with the best duration of sunlight available. Use grow lights to easily avoid this problem. These lights come in a variety of sizes and prices. Once you have decided where you will place your containers, you can have the lights placed (tube lights) or add a light bulb aimed at growing indoor plants.

Alternatively, if you get enough sun inside your home, especially around windows, a window box is the perfect container as you can grow several plants in it. You can even use tubs with at least 10–12 inches in depth. Once the container and lights are in place, you can mix the potting soil and fertilizer before adding it to the container of choice. Then you can add the seeds or transplants you want to grow indoors. Although the type of plant you grow is dependent on the container size, you will be limited to the area you can grow in when inside your home. Aim to grow plants that are dwarf versions or smaller plants. By growing these plants, you will be able to maintain them easier than their larger varieties. Ideal container sizes for growing indoors can vary from four inches for some herbs and microgreens, to as large as 14 inches for the larger vegetables or larger herbs, such as lemon verbena.

Plants that require support or a trellis, such as eggplants, tomatoes, or cucumbers, can be planted in the middle of a 5-gallon bucket, but they don't need to be alone. Plants such as lettuce, radishes, and small beets can be planted at the base of the stem to use more of the container. Alternatively, plant several different kinds of salad greens in a single container. This will give you a variety of tastes, textures, colors, and shapes within one container. Try combining arugula and a different loose-leaf or small-headed lettuce within a container. It'll be as if you are growing a salad bowl. You can even grow small-headed cabbage and small root vegetables such as beets and salad turnips. When growing beets, sow several seeds and then thin out the seedlings as they start to germinate.

Cabbage

Cabbages, as with other brassicas, are heavy nitrogen feeders. So, if you are planning on growing this plant indoors, ensure that you have ample nitrogen in your fertilizer. Avoid growing the larger varieties indoors. Stick to cultivars such as Red Ruby or even Chinese cabbage to get a more compact cabbage that tastes every bit as good as the larger varieties. Cabbage is best grown from seeds and needs to be watered well to ensure a compacted head.

Experiment with containers and light sources to see which best suit your needs in terms of space and what vegetables you want to grow. As the old proverb goes: Nothing ventured, nothing gained.

5

MORE HEALTHY EATING: MICROGREENS AND HERBS

U p to this point, mostly vegetables have been discussed but don't think for a minute that these unique gardening practices are limited to just growing them. Many edible herbs and microgreens also benefit from growing in raised beds, growing vertically, and within containers, especially well within containers.

HERBS

When deciding which herbs are best to grow, always consider the hardiness zone first. This is especially true when growing outdoors, as some herbs prefer more tropical conditions to thrive in—such as lemongrass. There are almost 100 different species of herbs that you can grow—and even more varieties. Each type has unique flavors and aromas that can be added to your garden to benefit it, or your home to brighten it. Herbs are truly wonderful and are some of the easiest plants to grow, especially when you know what you are doing.

Depending on what herbs you want to grow, you will need to ensure you know what they like. Some herbs prefer more water than others. Then some prefer to be in full sunlight, while others enjoy being in partial sunlight.

These plants are great to add to a raised bed to deter pests and attract beneficial insects with their blossoms. Plus, they rarely get infested with pests. They can be picked and used fresh in salads or other meals, or they can be dried and stored for later use. Just remember that dried herbs are more potent than fresh. You will need to use up to three times fewer dried herbs than fresh, otherwise, your meal may be spoiled.

Add herbs to containers or vertical gardens to keep their benefits around the garden without them invading the bed with potentially invasive roots. Or bring them indoors so you can enjoy their scents as you go about your day. Try planting a combination of herbs such as sage, cilantro, basil, oregano, and more, so you always have your preferred cooking herb on hand when you need it. No longer do you need to pay for herbs from the grocer, as they are growing in your very home!

Lifespans of Herbs

Herbs, unlike most vegetables, have set lifespans that can be described as annual, biennial, or perennial. Herbs that are described as annuals go through their entire lifecycle—seed, plant, flower, generating seed, and dying—within a single growing season, usually less than a year. These herbs are generally grown from seeds as some are too soft to survive transplanting easily. Herbs considered annuals include marjoram, basil, summer savory, fennel, dill, chervil, and cilantro.

Herbs that are biennials usually live 18–24 months before dying. The first year of their life is dedicated to producing foliage, while in the second year, the plant concentrates on creating flowers and seeds. These herbs are also grown from seeds and include watercress, parsley, sage, stevia, and angelica (wild celery). Herbs are sensitive to cooler temperatures, so if you want your biennials to survive winter, it is a good idea to bring them indoors. Otherwise, they won't live to produce flowers the following season if you have severe frost.

Perennial herbs can last for years if they are treated well and cared for. Its entire life cycle is completed within a single growing season, but after it produces flowers, the plant will later die back and become dormant. Once the seasons start to warm up, the plant will burst back into life and continue similarly to what it had the previous year. These herbs need more care than the annuals, as they like to spread and need the old stems removed just above ground level to promote better growth the next season. These herbs can be grown from seeds (although some tend to be more difficult than others), transplants, cuttings, and even root divisions. Herbs that fall into this category include mints (peppermint, spearmint, etc.), chives, oregano, rosemary, sage, tarragon (also known as estragon), thyme, and winter savory. These herbs can easily be grown indoors as well as outside.

Don't let their lifespans force you to make a decision over which herb is better than the next. No one herb is the best, and as long as you don't mind replanting from time to time, you can enjoy any herb you want in your raised, vertical, or container garden.

How to Grow Herbs From Seeds

Growing herbs from seeds can be difficult and time-consuming, and many people prefer to just buy their herbs as transplants and take care of them as young plants. However, there is something special about growing herbs from seed.

- The first thing you need to do is soak the seed you want to plant in water for 24 hours. Generally, seeds that are non-viable (won't become a plant) will float to the top, while those that sink are the better seeds.
- While the seeds are soaking, get the pots you want to use ready. Many people like to plant the seeds in a container that will hold the mature plant, while others like to start with something smaller such as eggshells or egg cartons.
- Add some potting mix—the same you use in your containers—to your preferred container you will be using for your herbs.

- The pots need to be ready to receive the seeds as soon as the soak is complete. After the 24-hour soak, the seeds need to be planted immediately, or they will go bad.
- Add the seed to the prepared container and lightly cover with some soil—no more than 0.25-inch. Don't pat it down as this will make it difficult for the seedlings to break through the surface.
- Fill a spray bottle with water and gently spray the top of the container.
- If planting several types of seeds in a container, be sure to mark what was planted where. Almost all seedlings look identical when they first sprout, so it will be difficult to tell them apart in the beginning.
- You can then add some cling film over the container to help retain moisture. Seeds are very delicate, so over or under-watering will kill them quickly.
- Move the container to a warm area—70 °F is ideal—in your home where it can get ample sunlight. Some seeds will need as much as 14–16 hours of sunlight to germinate and grow at their best.
- Mist the surface of the soil once in a while, just enough to keep it moist.

Depending on what herb you are growing, the germination can be as fast as 4 days (basil) or as long as 28 days (rosemary). It is also a good idea to add several seeds to the area where you would usually place a single seed. It is better to thin seedlings out as they grow, rather than having a dud seed that gives you nothing.

Transferring Seedlings

Certain herbs grow large, and if you choose the wrong container size or germinate seeds in smaller containers, you will need to transfer the seedling to something larger. Seedlings should only be transferred after the first two true leaves appear, which can be anywhere from one to four weeks. You need to ensure that the roots don't get root bound, so in smaller containers, you may have to transplant them into larger containers earlier than anticipated. If a plant becomes root bound, remove it from the container and gently roll the root bundle between your hands to loosen the roots. Once they are loose, you can add the plant to its new container.

Once a transplant is made—after the true leaves have appeared—the young plant doesn't need as much attention as the seed did. Herbs don't like to be watered often, and some prefer to have their soil dry a little between watering sessions. It is better to water every other day rather than a weekly or daily soaking. Know which herbs like what watering conditions.

Making Cuttings

The woodier herbs (rosemary, oregano, etc.) can be propagated from cuttings of mature plants:

- Look for a long stem and cut it off just above the ground.
- Remove several leaves around the base of the stem.
- Place the cutting in a container with moist soil.
- It is important to keep the soil moist and in a shaded area to give the cutting a chance to grow new roots.
- Continue to water gently for about two weeks.
- Congratulations! You have just created a new plant from a cutting.

After a few more weeks, the transplant will be ready to be moved out into the garden or a more permanent container.

Understanding Herbs

To get the most out of the herbs you are growing, you need to understand their natures and what they need to grow at their optimum. Most herbs like the soil to be slightly acidic to neutral, while it shouldn't be too fertile. Parsley is one of the few herbs that prefer highly organic soil.

Drainage is vital for most herbs as they don't like to be in high moisture environments. That said, there are exceptions for this rule, mainly with mint, angelica, and lovage. The woodier the herb, the more likely it will prefer sparse waterings instead of being soaked. Try to group herbs and other plants with similar water needs. This way the watering strategy you use will best be optimized for what you are growing, especially in a raised bed or large container.

The more sunlight an herb receives, the more fragrant it will be. Plant in areas receiving a minimum of 6–8 hours of sunlight. This is not to say partial sunlight is bad for herbs, just that their aroma and flavors will be less potent.

Not all herbs like to be planted as transplants or seeds. Rosemary is particularly tricky when trying to grow from seed. Meanwhile, dill, cilantro, and fennel can be damaged during a transplant, preventing them from growing at their best. The standard rule of herbs is that if it is a softer herb, it is best to not transplant it.

Herbs come with a variety of benefits to you and your garden. They contain minerals and vitamins essential to your health, plus their aromas deter many kinds of pests that would destroy your crops. Their flowers attract beneficial insects and add to the beauty of your garden. For the most part, insects will avoid the more pungent herbs but will devour the softer kinds. You are likely to frequently see aphids or spider mites affecting your woodier herbs and caterpillars on the softer varieties.

Herbs are right at home wherever there is soil be that in a raised bed, a container, or even indoors. As long as you follow all the advice outlined in the earlier chapters, these plants will thrive wherever you want to plant them.

You will mostly benefit from herbs earlier in the growing season, especially those which prefer cooler temperatures. As soon as herbs become stressed—as with high temperatures—they will start to bolt. This is when the plant is convinced that it is dying and to save its genetic material for the future, it starts to flower earlier than normal. Although many herb flowers are stunning and beneficial, it usually spells the end of the growing season of that particular herb. As the plant puts more energy into producing seeds, the leaves tend to change in shape, color, and aroma. The stems also become woodier. This change in the plant results in the leaves becoming bitter or less flavorful, in essence, ruining the herb. This may not be a concern for perennials, but it's a disaster for an annual as it cannot recover in time to produce new aromatic leaves before the end of its growing season. If you are after the seeds, this is no problem. However, if you aim to harvest the leaves, you will need to put a stop to the bolting process. Luckily this is easy to do.

When inspecting your herbs, take care in noting any flowering buds. These should be removed as soon as they are noticed. However, plants may bolt because of the heat, and you will need to deal with that before the problem can be solved. Move the plant to a cooler area, or offer it shade with some cloth or taller plants. Adding mulch around the plant can help lower the temperature of the soil. Although herbs rarely need fertilizer, if adding some, ensure that it contains low levels of phosphorus, as this promotes flower development.

Once the bolting process has been halted, the plant will concentrate more on growing, rather than creating seeds. Resulting in a larger and bushier plant. However, if you are aiming to collect seeds, you need to be cautious, as many herbs are self-seeders and will add their seeds to the area where they grow. This will lead to a contaminated raised bed when growing in one.

Harvesting Herbs

Herbs can be harvested at any point while they are growing. Individual leaves can be snipped off or whole stems collected. The best time to harvest is just before the plant starts to flower, just as the dew starts to dry on the leaves.

When collecting from annuals and biennials, wait until the stems are at least 4–6 inches long. Use sharp scissors or garden shears and cut above the last set of leaves on the stem. With perennials, you can either remove the leaf tips or up to a third of the length of a stem from one part of the plant. This area should be allowed time to recover, while a different section is utilized later. Never collect more than a third of the length of the plant, or it will take too long for it to recover.

When collecting seeds, wait until the flower head appears and starts to go brown. The seeds are now mature, but the flower head is also ready to open. Use caution when collecting to prevent self-seeding. Add the flowering heads to a paper bag and gently shake to release all the seeds. These seeds will need to be dried and stored away in an airtight container until you are ready to plant them.

Preservation and Storage

Once picked, herbs don't last very long. You can extend their shelf-life by adding the stems to a glass of water in the fridge or wrapping the woodier stems in damp tissue paper. However, this will only buy you a few days at most. The best way to preserve herbs is to dry or freeze them.

Dried herbs are just as good as fresh herbs, but they last significantly longer. They can last up to a year before their potency starts to degrade. By drying your herbs, you'll never have to run to the store for herbs again. There are a variety of ways you can dry the plants.

The easiest is to air dry them as this requires no tools. Once you have harvested the stems, tie them together in a bundle. You want to keep the bundles—about 5–10 stems—in an area that is cool and receives good airflow with no sun. This technique can take several weeks, but by the end, you have fragrant, dried herbs, ready for use. You'll need to keep an eye on the bundles as they dry. As moisture evaporates, the stems will shrink, and there is a chance the bundles loosen. Once completely dry, remove the leaves from the stem and store them in airtight containers.

You can also air-dry leaves only, but you will need some paper towels. After washing and patting dry the leaves, add them in a single layer between two paper towels. Next, place it in an area with good air circulation away from the sun. Now and again, check that the leaves are drying out.

If these techniques take too long, consider using a microwave to dry the herbs. Herbs should be thoroughly washed and dried before starting, as you don't want to cook them. Remove the leaves and place them between two paper towels. Place in the microwave and heat the leaves at the highest setting for 30 seconds. Remove the paper from the microwave. If the leaves aren't dry and crispy to touch, gently turn them over and heat for another 30 seconds. Continue this until the leaves crumble when rubbed between two fingers. Allow the herbs to cool down in an area with good airflow before adding them to an airtight container. This technique works best with woodier herbs such as oregano and rosemary.

There are other tools you can use to dry your herbs, such as air fryers (135 °F for thirty minutes), an oven (125 °F for four hours), or a multicooker such as an instant pot (125 °F for three and a half hours). The main thing to remember is that the leaves need to be placed as a single layer to prevent them from sticking to each other and not drying properly.

When storing herbs, the size of the container is important. You don't want to place the dried herbs in large containers, as this can welcome moisture and, therefore, mold. You may be tempted to dry a lot of herbs, but rather dry enough to fill a few glass jars—such as baby food jars—which are easy to store away from moisture and sunlight. Dried herbs should never be added to the fridge or freezer and should be labeled with the date and the name of the herb. After about a year, test the herbs to see if they still have the potency you expect of them. If you're happy with the aroma of the herbs, then continue to use them. If not, dispose of them and make new dried herbs.

Drying herbs isn't your only way to preserve these plants. They can also be frozen. Delicate herbs such as basil, fennel, and cilantro don't dry well, but when frozen, they can last up to six months in your freezer. Wash the leaves well and pat dry. Add the leaves in a single layer on a freezer-safe tray or cookie sheet. Freeze overnight before placing the individually frozen leaves in a freezer-safe, airtight container, or ziplock baggie. Remember once you remove these leaves from the freezer, they will defrost and become mush. This technique can also be used with whole stems of woodier herbs.

You can also freeze the herbs in water or oil. This can be done by adding the cleaned leaves or a pureed herb mixture to ice cube trays. Only add a couple of leaves or 1–2 teaspoons of the mixture, depending on the cube size. When deciding to freeze in oil or water, it comes down to what you want to use the herbs in.

Herbs frozen in water are generally added to soups and stews, while those added to oil can be used in sauces for meals or in soapmaking. Herbs which are best frozen in water include mint, parsley, and basil. For oil, the best herbs are basil, thyme, and oregano. Unlike the herbs frozen as is, those frozen in water or oil can last significantly longer, but you are likely to use them in your cooking and will need to make new cubes frequently.

Some Useful Herbs

You are spoiled for choice when it comes to planting herbs, but here are some of my favorites that are perfect for beginners.

Rosemary is a perennial with an attractive blue flower that prefers warmer climates and moderate humidity. This plant isn't overly fond of moisture and thrives in full sun. It is notoriously difficult to grow this herb from seeds, and it is best to plant it as a transplant. This highly aromatic herb works well in stews or teas to help with memory.

Mint is a voracious perennial grower. The only way to keep it under control is to give it a container all for itself. Mint can be grown from transplants or cuttings, and it prefers high moisture areas. Plants from the mint family are recognized by their square stem.

Parsley is a biennial that is best recognized as garnishing on a plate. Ignored by most, this herb is a must in a garden as its addition to meals gives you a boost in iron and vitamins C and A. The seeds like to grow in slightly acidic (pH 6) organic-rich soil when they can experience the full sun.

Sage is a perennial known for its grayish-green leaves and a flower spike that can be pink, purple, blue, or white. It hates standing in water but likes frequent watering, so it will need well-draining soil to keep it happy. It cannot be grown with mint. It grows best from seeds or cuttings. Great as a fresh, frozen, or dried herb in many dishes.

Chives are technically an allium (onion) but are treated as an herb. It is recognized by its spiky green leaves and pom-pom-like purple flowers. This herb is a prolific seeder, and as soon as the flower is noted, it needs to be picked. Thankfully it is edible, so it doesn't go to waste. Not only is this perennial delicious in a meal, but it's also known for its insect-deterring nature. As it grows, its small bulb is pushed to the surface, so be sure to add some mulch to protect it from onion maggots. When storing this herb for future use, freeze it, as drying it will lessen its flavor.

MICROGREENS

Microgreens are tiny greens (practically seedlings) that can be grown anywhere you have space. Most people like to grow them indoors, but they can also be grown in containers on porches and balconies. Little time is wasted growing these plants to reach full maturity, as they are eaten early in their life due to their high nutritional value and ease of harvest. There are a wide variety of vegetables and herbs that can be grown as microgreens.

Microgreens are planted in high concentrations over a small area to give a dense growth of plants that often resembles a mat. Germination is done in the dark, but once the seeds sprout, they will require adequate lighting.

Benefits

Microgreens offer the same benefits as vegetables, but at a fraction of the time it requires to grow the fully mature plant. There is very little fuss in growing microgreens, as they can grow anywhere, and anyone can grow them once they have containers ready for seeds. Microgreens are packed with flavor, fiber, and many types of vitamins including C, B, E, and K as well as the minerals manganese, magnesium, copper, potassium, zinc, and iron. They are also full of antioxidants. Growing microgreens will be far cheaper than buying them in-store, as they don't have a long shelf-life. They are a great healthy food that can always be on hand to be added to anything from a salad to a smoothie.

Microgreens grow fast, and if you stagger planting, you will easily have several mats of greens you can harvest once they are ready. Generally, you don't need to control the climate when growing inside, but you'll need to have a sheltered area for the microgreens if you are growing them outside. The best part of microgreens is that they rarely suffer from plant diseases and insect feeding activity, as they don't spend a long time growing. However, due to the closeness at which they grow, there is a chance of fungal infections, which can destroy an entire tray if you aren't careful.

How to Grow Microgreens

To grow microgreens, you will need some equipment. Unlike the other plants discussed in this book, you want to keep the root systems of your microgreens as shallow as possible. Get several shallow (1–1.5 inch depth) seed trays with drainage holes to grow your microgreens. You will also need

- various seeds of choice (mustard, sunflower, peas, etc.): Aim to use several types in several trays. Generally, it is encouraged to get good quality seeds, but older seeds are also usable. The seeds will be so densely sown that a few duds won't affect the whole tray.
- spray bottle
- clean water (vital)
- large tray in which seed trays can fit in
- growth medium: There is a variety you can use, such as peat mixtures or coconut coir (fiber). You can also use potting soil. Alternatively, a growth mat can also be used. These mats can be made of cotton or hemp.
- sharp harvesting tool (scissors)
- measuring spoons and a scale: You will need these to measure the weight of seeds per growing tray you will fill.
- fertilizer (optional)

- grow lights (optional)

Once you have the equipment ready, you will need to work out the seed density required per tray with the microgreen seeds you'll be growing. Each seed type will have its preferred growing density given the space in the growing tray. Use these tips to grow microgreens efficiently:

- Choose the microgreens you want to grow.
- Use a microgreen seed density calculator (many available online) to determine the total weight of the particular seed you want to grow in combination with the size of the tray you are using.
- Some hard-shelled seeds such as peas or sunflowers will need to be soaked overnight to aid in their germination. Do this before prepping the seed trays.
- Fill the shallow trays with the preferred growth medium.
- Add clean water to the large tray and place the seed trays in the water.
- Allow the water to soak up through the growing medium until the top of the seed trays is moist to the touch. This is essential as the moist growth medium will help with the

germination of the seeds placed on it.

- Once the seed trays are moist enough, remove them from the water tray and allow excess water to drain away. Note how long this takes as you will need the approximate time it takes for later use.

- Add the predetermined weight of seeds to the trays. Spread them out as equally as possible. The best spacing is ⅛–¼ inch between each seed. Press the seeds down lightly into the growing medium. You can use another dry tray to achieve this.

- Generally, there is no need to cover the seeds with the growth medium—although some people who use soil will add ⅛ of an inch over the seeds. Whether you add soil over the top of the seeds or not, seeds must be protected from heat and direct sunlight. Keep the seed trays in a dark, cool area for a few days to allow the seeds to germinate. Use the spray bottle frequently—once to twice a day—to keep the seeds and the surface of the growth medium moist.

- The trays can be covered by the water tray to keep them in the dark as they germinate. This should take about 3–7 days, maybe a little longer for harder-shelled seeds.

BEGINNER'S FIELD GUIDE TO RAISED BED, CONTAIN... | 123

- Once all the seedlings are about ½ an inch in height, the cover can be removed.
- Move the seed tray to an area with adequate sunlight, roughly 4–8 hours daily will be sufficient.
- Mold is a big problem with growing microgreens and can be avoided with the correct watering strategy.
- Instead of misting from the top-down, and getting the leaves wet, add the seed trays to the larger tray filled with water and allow the growth medium to soak up the moisture. It should take roughly as long as it took to soak the seed trays before adding the seeds.
- Remove the trays from the water and allow the growth medium to drain the excess water before placing it back in the sunny area.
- When concerned about microgreens appearing too wet, open a window to increase the air circulation. This should help with some of the evaporation and lower the chances of mold developing.

If you are new to growing microgreens and don't know when the different life cycles of a plant occur, keep a notebook handy. Write down the dates of when you start, when you water, and what the seeds do. You can even add notes about the taste and flavor of the micro-greens after you harvest them. By keeping these notes on hand, you will be armed with more knowledge the next time you try to grow microgreens.

How to Harvest Microgreens

When the seeds germinate, they produce their first leaves known as cotyledons. These are not true leaves, and you shouldn't harvest your microgreens when you notice them. Microgreens should only be harvested once their first true leaves start to show. The time it takes for the first true leaves to appear is dependent on the plant you are growing, as it can take anywhere from about ten days to two weeks.

This is not to say you can't harvest the plants as soon as they have grown into their cotyledons. However, if you do, you won't be eating a microgreen but rather a sprout. Sprouts can be eaten root and all, while micro-greens aren't.

- Once the microgreens are ready to be harvested, take sharp scissors and cut them off just above the surface of the growth medium.
- Wash the microgreens before adding them to whatever meals you want to.
- If you want the microgreens to last longer after harvest, add them to a glass of water in the

fridge before washing them. These are delicate plants, and washing them can cause damage, resulting in irreversible wilt in a matter of hours. By cutting the microgreens, you stop their development, but by adding them to the water in the fridge, you increase their longevity.

- Once all the microgreens have been harvested from the growth medium, the medium can be added to your compost, and the trays washed to be reused for the next batch.

By having several trays with seeds sowed at different times, you can create an endless source of fresh greens that can be grown anywhere. Microgreen harvesting is a once-off harvest. Once the greens have been cut away from the roots, they will not grow again.

Best Microgreens to Grow

As long as the plant is edible, it is likely that the microgreen will also be edible. Microgreens are divided into groups according to their seed size. Large microgreen seeds are the easiest to sow evenly. However, some of these seeds may require a soak to help them germinate easier. These are also the type of seeds that need some weight to keep them in contact with the growing medium. It is best to add another tray on top while the seeds are in the dark. The seeds in this category include beets, fennel, parsley, and cilantro.

The medium microgreen-sized seeds are easier to sow than the smaller seeds but not as easy as larger types. Some of these seeds contain tough hulls and may need soaking, but this isn't true for all seeds. Seeds such as chia might need soaking, but mustard, spinach, and radish might not. If unsure, soak all seeds for a few hours before placing them on the growth medium. It isn't necessary to place a weight on the seeds as they grow.

The small microgreen seeds can be difficult to sow evenly, and there is no trick other than experience when it comes to getting the perfect sow. Generally, seeds from this category are the most flavorful, though there are exceptions to this rule. Alfalfa grows well as a microgreen and has many vitamins and minerals, but it tends to lack flavor. Luckily, you can grow mint, celery, sage, and thyme to make up for the lack of flavor.

If it is edible and you can grow it, consider it a microgreen. Test a variety of vegetables and herbs to see which best suits your palate.

6

OH THOSE LITTLE PESTS— GARDEN MAINTENANCE

P ests and weeds are animals and plants you don't want in your gardening space, even if they are beneficial in some way. You don't want lavender sprouting where you have carrots. Luckily, there are many ways that you can deal with unwanted plants and animals. Even better, none of these ways have to be over-the-counter toxins that are not only harmful to the things you're trying to get rid of but also to the rest of the environment. Most outdoor gardens—less frequently indoor gardens—are a haven for many insects, animals, viruses, bacteria, and unwanted plants that want to utilize the space you have created. Nip it in the bud before it can become a problem.

INSECTS

The first thing you need to realize is that not all insects are harmful. Without insects, there would be no way for most of our plants to be pollinated and produce crops. Insects can be divided into two groups: helpful (beneficial) and harmful. The best way to know which falls into what group is to educate yourself. Although not everyone can be an entomologist, there are plenty of field guides with handy pictures to help you identify any insect that comes into your garden. Even if you don't want to use a field guide, there are many people online who are willing to help you.

Even after you identify helpful insects, they can still be problems. Take butterflies, for example. They can pollinate flowers as adults, but their larva can cause havoc in a garden. Similarly, bees are deadly to those who have allergies to their stings.

To attract beneficial insects over the harmful kind, you need to consider what they need to thrive. Insects that pollinate are attracted to bright blossoms that have strong aromas. Predatory insects (ladybirds) or parasitoids (insects that parasitize), such as several wasp species, need to have access to their food supply, such as caterpillars or aphids.

Most gardeners won't experience an infestation of harmful insects, as a well-balanced natural environment keeps the number of harmful insects at bay. However, when there is a disturbance in the environment, it can cause infestations to occur. The best way to deal with these is to keep an eye on your garden and note what is visiting it.

Certain pests appear to coincide with different times of the year. Because of this, you may need to adjust your planting strategy to avoid a potential infestation. Pests such as squash vine borers—which appear from May to June—can cause a lot of damage to butternut, but this can be avoided by planting later in the season to avoid them. Keep a notebook on which pest species are likely to appear during the year, so you can be ready for them next year.

Not all plants are susceptible to attack from insects. Some plants are hardier or are resistant to feeding damage from specific species of insects. If you know you are in an area that gets visited frequently by a certain pest, look to planting resistant crops.

The best way to prevent insects from damaging your crops is to place a barrier between them and your plants. Items such as hoop houses and row covers are perfect. However, this also stops insects from pollinating the blossoms. If this is the route you want to go, you will need to teach yourself how to hand-pollinate your plants to still get the crops you want.

When you first notice signs of an insect feeding on your crops, try to identify the culprit! The best time to look for pests is in the morning. Turn over leaves to find them. Once found, they can be removed by hand, squirted with some water to dislodge them, or a length of sticky tape can be used to collect small insects such as aphids. If you don't want these insects to come back, drop them in some hot water, as it'll kill them instantly.

Lastly, don't assume what you grow in your various gardens will be as perfect as what is found in stores. Commercial farms spend billions trying to curb damage by insects, and you never see the fruit or vegetables that aren't perfect. Lastly, appreciate what you get from your garden, even if the leaves are chewed by a caterpillar, or there is a worm in the middle of your cabbage. Wash it, cut it out, and carry on enjoying the hard work you put into your garden

Natural Pest Control

There are many natural ways to deal with insects without adding poisons to the environment. Your best bet is to turn to nature itself. There are a variety of birds, reptiles, and mammals that are perfect for the job. To attract these animals (sparrows, lizards, and bats) to your outside garden, you want to make it as inviting as possible. As humans need water, food, and shelter to survive, so do animals. As long as you're providing extra food and water on top of all the bugs they can eat, these animals are less likely to turn to your garden for a snack.

Companion Planting

Your next step goes hand-in-hand with planning your raised bed or large container gardens. Companion planting not only benefits the growth of the plant but also protects those around it. Alliums are a great deterrent against many insects. Plant onions, garlic, or even shallots in rows between your other crops, or around the edge of the bed.

Also, consider some flowers around the area as companion plants to your vegetables and herbs. Chrysanthemums are perfect against spider mites (which will affect indoor and outdoor plants) and Japanese beetles. The flower is also known to guard against lice, ants, and even roaches.

When planting beans and potatoes together, both plants benefit and protect each other. The beans add extra nitrogen to the soil and secrete a chemical that deters the Colorado potato beetle. Meanwhile, the potatoes secrete a chemical that deters the Mexican bean beetle from finding your beans appetizing.

Rosemary in pots around a raised bed can benefit three different vegetable groups. Its aroma deters carrot flies, bean beetles, and cabbage moths from trying to get to your veggies. If you have a cat, why not plant catnip yourself and save on buying it? Not only will your cat be happy, but the plant protects zucchini and cucumber from the dreaded cucumber beetles. There are many ways to pair plants as companions. With some research before planting, you can come up with the ideal planting strategy to protect your crops.

Homemade Deterrents

There are a variety of homemade sprays that either target a specific insect or any it comes into contact with. Japanese beetles can be persuaded to leave green beans alone if you add some garden lime to the plant and fruit. The brassica-loving cabbage looper is a major problem for people who grow high numbers of different kinds of brassica. To stop this insect, add three teaspoons of cayenne pepper to a quart of water and mix well. Add the mixture to a spray bottle and spray it on the base of the stem, the foliage, and all branching stems.

Another annoying insect that not only damages your plant but spreads many diseases is the aphid. These insects will suck the life out of your plant in a matter of days if the infestation is high enough. To deal with these pests, add two chilis, a small onion, and a green pepper to a blender. Blend until you have a smooth mixture. Add a quart of water and mix well. Strain the solids and add the liquid to a spray bottle. Spray directly onto the insect.

Alternatively, you can keep a 2% dish soap solution on hand at all times in a spray bottle. Insect bodies have a fine layer of wax. Once this waxy layer is disturbed, it becomes more susceptible to damage, disease, and dehydration. By spraying the soapy solution directly onto eggs and insects, it disrupts the waxy membrane, causing the insects to succumb more readily. This is an all-purpose solution that can be used on all insects.

None of these deterrents are harmful to people. As long as you wash the leaves and vegetables well before eating, you shouldn't have any negative effects.

When nature is no longer able to deal with the insects on your crops, it is your time to step in and help. There are many ways to deal with unwanted guests, but before you reach for a poison, read its label carefully. Some poisons have a specific duration that you can use during the plants' development. Other poisons are only meant to be used on ornamental plants rather than fruiting types. When these poisons are incorrectly used, this is when not only the natural environment suffers but also those in your home—people and animals included.

LARGER PESTS

It isn't only insects that can become a pest in the garden. Whether you are growing indoors or outdoors, there is always something that wants to eat what you plant. What larger animals may affect your garden is dependent on where you live. Not everyone has bears, but most people will be affected by rodents, such as rats, mice, and squirrels. Once you know what kinds of larger pest species you have in the vicinity, you can take steps to stop them.

Firstly, you want to prevent them from finding your garden hospitable. Remove garden waste or unprotected food lying around. Look for areas that are great for hiding in and get rid of them. A clean garden prevents rabbits from finding a place to bed down. Once completed, you'll need to implement one or several control methods that best suit the pest affecting your garden.

Control Damage Naturally

When you have a large enough garden with several raised beds, the best way to protect your crops is to ring the property with a fence. This fence should be high enough to prevent deer from jumping over and be partially buried to stop rabbits digging under. The material used should be of such a nature that it cannot be climbed easily by raccoons or squirrels. The fence can also be electrified, although this can increase the cost more than what most people are willing to pay.

Pets such as cats and dogs—maybe even the occasional toddler—make great protectors for your crops. Cats can curb the number of rodents, while dogs will bark to warn off any larger animal that wanders onto your property.

On a smaller scale, you can use cloches over individual plants or whole raised beds and containers. These small cages are made of wire mesh and create a barrier that most animals cannot get through. However, the larger the animal you want to stop, the more heavy-duty the cloche will need to be.

Some repellents can be used. Many pest species that destroy gardens are considered prey items. Due to this, they tend to avoid areas that smell like a predator. Some garden centers sell the urine of certain predatory animals that can be used as a deterrent. Alternatively, some blood along the edges of your property will work just as well. However, wild animals will eventually learn it is a trick and still enter your property. When these animals start to get brave, switch up the repellant you use. Think of visual and auditory repellents that could work. Something as simple as a piece of tinfoil on a string can deter some birds. While an automated sprinkler system or motion sensor light will frighten any nighttime visitor.

Sometimes the animal presence cannot be dealt with, and this is when you may need to spend the money to employ someone from animal control. They can handle the legality of dealing with trapping and disposing of any problem animal that is more than just a nuisance. With luck, these people will lay live traps to catch squirrels, rabbits, possums, and even chipmunks. This way a living animal is caught and removed from your property.

WEEDS

Simply put, weeds are undesirable plants among those that are desirable. Common weeds usually grow quicker than the other plants and can quickly out-compete them for resources. In a well-groomed garden, weeds stand out like a sore thumb, especially in container gardens. Weeds are prolific seeders and will contaminate the area around them. They are a nuisance, but luckily with some consistent weeding, they are easy to control.

Control Naturally

When growing in raised beds or containers, the soil is light and fluffy, making weeding significantly easier than in a standard garden. So why bother with purchased poisons?

When placing a raised bed on an existing piece of grass or lot, you must control the weeds before the bed is added. This can be done by digging up the sod or even applying a layer of clear or black plastic over the area. Once the plastic is sealed, you can use the sun to kill off any weeds and grass below it. This can also be achieved by adding some landscaper's fabric or newspaper before adding the raised bed. By cutting off the weed's source of light, it will eventually die.

Weeding is as simple as gripping the stem just above ground level and pulling. Unfortunately, some weed species have caught onto this trick, and when pulled up, sometimes they leave pieces of their root system behind. These pieces can then generate a new weed later. Thankfully, once uprooted several times, the recurrence of weeds is less. When deciding to use this approach, ensure that you are pulling the weed before it gets a chance to form a flower head and seeds. Otherwise, you may be too late as it could have already spread its seeds.

The addition of mulch to your raised bed helps to smother newly growing weeds—some of which you may not even recognize as weeds early in their growth. However, if you don't want to mulch, plan your planting so that the foliage of the growing plants blocks out the sun, preventing newly developing weeds from gaining a roothold.

When weeds are particularly bad in a raised bed, you can apply vinegar or boiling water to the offending weed. You shouldn't do this in a container as both these solutions can cause damage to neighboring plants. Industrial strength vinegar (20% acetic acid) works best on weeds when sprayed on the stems and leaves. The vinegar needs to be applied several times to lower the occurrence of the weeds and their spread. Extreme caution should be taken when spraying this vinegar, as unlike kitchen vinegar, it will cause damage to your eyes, skin, and even lungs. Avoid oversaturating the ground below the plant, as this will affect other plants in the general vicinity.

Boiling water is used the same way as vinegar but is somewhat less hazardous to your lungs and eyes. This solution will quickly kill foliage but may take a while to kill off weeds with deep tap roots. Similar to vinegar, avoid having too much boiling water reaching the ground as it can affect other plants close by.

If you are still plagued by weeds, add two tablespoons of rubbing alcohol to a quart of water. Pour into a spray bottle and apply it to the leaves. This may kill back the foliage, but be careful as this will also kill the foliage of unintended plants if they are accidentally sprayed as well.

Green Garden Enemies

Some of the most common weeds that will invade your beds, and possibly your containers, are those that spread through creeping or producing seeds that are spread through the wind.

Dandelions are recognized by their yellow flowers, puffball seed heads, and deeply toothed leaves. This plant is particularly troublesome in lawns, but your raised bed or containers won't be spared as the seeds are carried by the wind. It has a deep tap root that will make removing this weed a pain.

Canada thistles also spread through wind and will grow anywhere they land. This plant is recognized by its purple flower and prickly, serrated leaves. Remove with caution.

Pigweed is a stunning plant that grows tall and looks similar to amaranth when it grows. The problem is that the flower, which it is well known for, causes it to spread like wildfire with the number of seeds it produces. Remove this plant before the flower appears.

Purslane is a succulent with small, fleshy leaves that spread through thousands of seeds and parts of its leaves. Even a small piece of a leaf you removed from somewhere in your garden can propagate in a raised bed within days. If you have this plant in your garden, be very careful when removing it.

Chickweed grows as a mat of tiny, green, tear-shaped leaves with tiny, white flowers. This plant loves well-watered areas and acts as a reservoir—a haven—for insects and diseases through winter.

Remember that these plants are only considered weeds when they're growing in areas you don't want them. Some of them are not only edible but even good for you. Dandelion greens are sweet earlier in the year and grow more bitter as they age. They are high in vitamin C and can be grown as a microgreen. Even clover can be grown as a microgreen and offers a wide range of vitamins and minerals. So, before you pull up a so-called "weed," try to identify it and see if you can use it instead.

INCREASING GARDEN HEALTH

The best way to avoid pests and weeds from showing up in your garden is to maintain its health. When the environment in the garden is disturbed, it can lead to stressed plants. These plants then become susceptible to disease and insect attacks. A healthy garden is in balance with nature.

The day you start gardening, you're disturbing the environment with what you're doing and bringing into your property. Check the soil and particularly your transplants. Nothing should be contaminated with disease or insects. You can even check the roots of the transplants to ensure they are disease-free.

Many gardeners want to make their own compost. The problem is many can't recognize good from poor compost. As organic material decays, it increases in temperature, killing harmful bacteria. However, when composting isn't done correctly, these high temperatures are never reached, resulting in pathogens remaining alive. These pathogens can then later be incorporated into raised beds or containers, spreading disease. If your compost doesn't have an earthy smell or looks slimy, it's best to avoid it.

Know the different disease-carrying insects. Most fall into the Heteroptera group, which is made up of the order Hemiptera, and the suborder Homoptera. Aphids, whiteflies, leafhoppers, etc., have piercing-sucking mouthparts that suck plants dry and can spread many diseases from plant to plant. Once you have identified the pest, address it quickly. The longer the plant is under attack, the more susceptible it becomes.

When dealing with a diseased plant, remove it from the garden to prevent the spread of disease. This extends to the last harvest in fall. Remove all plant debris to where you will compost, or dispose of it correctly. By keeping the debris in the garden bed or container, you are welcoming diseases and insects not yet apparent to overwinter safely.

Sadly, some plant cultivars are more susceptible to disease and insect predation. If you know you are in an area that gets a certain disease or insect, invest in purchasing seeds that are resistant to attack. Normally, this information is noted on seed packets. Alternatively, get seed catalogs or speak to experienced gardeners to get their advice.

Other things that can stress your garden are incorrect watering strategies, watering from the top, and incorrect spacing. You cannot group plants that need high volumes of water with those that don't, as it'll lead to problems. These problems are also noted when plants are watered from the top. Wet foliage in high humidity causes fungal diseases to develop and spread. This can be made worse when plants are grown too close together. When too many plants are grown in a small area, they are forced to compete for water, sunlight, and food. This increases the stress the plants experience, and they become more susceptible to disease, spreading it throughout the bed or container. Practice thinning out seedlings or trimming leaves of neighboring plants to ensure enough space for all in the bed.

COMMON PROBLEMS

To help you identify some of the common diseases and insects that can affect some of your beginner crops, here is a handy table to help you.

Plants	Problems
Peppers	**Insect** • Aphids are small, green, pear-shaped insects that don't have wings early in their development. These pests are found under leaves, but in high concentrations will be found all over the plant. • The feeding action of these insects causes leaves to yellow and become misshapen over time. They also secrete a sticky substance known as honeydew, which can cause the growth of black sooty mold. • They can be controlled with 2% dish soap solution or squashing when noticed. • Other insect pests include tomato hornworms, Colorado potato beetles, flea beetles, and leaf miners. **Disease** • Bacterial leaf spot causes black or rust-colored spots between the veins of the leaves. These spots appear wet at first but will later dry, causing holes to form in the leaves. • Leaves may also turn yellow and become distorted before wilting and falling off. • Cankers can develop on the stem. • The best treatment is to remove the affected area and destroy it. Avoid watering overhead. • Other diseases include anthracnose, blossom-end rot, and cucumber mosaic virus.

Tomatoes	**Insect**
	• As a caterpillar, the tomato hornworm is large, green, and has diagonal yellow-white stripes over its spiracles (breathing pores). At the end of the caterpillar is what appears to be a stinger. The adult is a moth that varies from dusky brown to gray.
	• The caterpillar eats the foliage, leaving only bare stems when in high concentrations.
	• The best way to deal with this pest is to handpick them and destroy any eggs found on the underside of leaves. Row covers will also protect your plants.
	• Other insect pests include aphids, many types of caterpillars, and flea beetles.
	Disease
	• Blossom-end rot causes the ends of the fruit to darken before becoming sunk in as the fruit breaks down.
	• This disease affects any plants that have a deficiency of calcium. This can be caused by under or over-watering, making it more difficult to absorb calcium.
	• It can also be caused by the pH of the soil being incorrect for the plant, the soil being too high in nitrogen, or the roots having been damaged.
	• To prevent an entire harvest from being affected, add fertilizer with a higher calcium content.
	• Other diseases include early and light blight, mosaic virus, fusarium wilt, and powdery mildew.
Zucchini	**Insect**
	• Squash bugs look like a longer version of a stink bug and come in browns, grays, or a mixture of black and red.
	• This bug weakens the plant by sucking up its juices, spreading disease, and causing a lower yield.
	• It's best to protect crops in early summer by adding row covers.
	• Adults and eggs can be dislodged with a spray of water.
	• Other insects include squash vine borer, cucumber beetles, and aphids.
	Disease
	• Powdery mildew presents as a fuzzy white fungal growth that is noticed above and below the leaf. In time the leaves will wilt and fall from the plant, spreading the fungal spores.
	• Affected leaves should be removed and destroyed. Don't water from above and trim the foliage to encourage better airflow.
	• Other diseases include blossom-end rot, bacterial wilt, and downy mildew.

Cucumbers	**Insect** • Cucumber beetles are inch-long beetles that are oval-shaped that can be yellow with black spots or stripes, while others are green or red with spots. The larval form is less than an inch-long yellow worm with a black or dark brown head. • The adults tend to eat holes through leaves and blossoms, while the larvae eat the roots and stems. • Protect crops with row covers, mulch, and handpick any adults noted. • Other insects to watch are aphids, whiteflies, and squash bugs. **Disease** • Downy mildew is similar to powdery mildew, but the fungal growth grows under the leaves in colored clusters of white, purple, or gray. The top part of the leaves develops angular yellow spots before turning brown and distorting. Eventually, the leaves will drop from the plant. • Don't water overhead and use resistant cultivars. Remove any affected part of the plant and destroy it. • Other diseases include anthracnose, blossom-end rot, cucumber mosaic virus, and powdery mildew.
Beans	**Insect** • Cutworms are rarely noticed until your plants start wilting and falling over. The larvae, which live just below the soil, chew through the stems as they feed. The worms vary from green to brown and will curl into a C-shape when disturbed. The adult moths are brown with darker patches over their wings. • Protect the stems by adding a cardboard or paper collar to prevent the larva from chewing them. Remove any larvae you notice by hand. • Other insects include aphids, cucumber beetles, Japanese beetles, leafhoppers, and Mexican bean beetles. **Disease** • Anthracnose is a fungal infection that causes spots of varying color (yellow, brown, purple, and even black) on leaves. When affecting pods and stems, the spots are generally black, resulting in sunken holes that eventually start to rot. • This is generally caused by overwatering and watering from above. Destroy affected crops and rotate beans out for a few seasons. • Other diseases include mosaic virus, powdery mildew, and white mold.

Lettuce	**Insect** • Earwigs are easily identified by their pincer-like tail. This insect likes to hide in garden debris and will eat holes through stems and leaves. • Remove any garden debris and lay earwig traps. Take a sardine can and bury it in the bed. Add 0.5-inch of fish oil. This attracts and drowns them. • Other insects to watch for are aphids, cutworms, and whiteflies. **Disease** • Lettuce mosaic virus causes leaves to become discolored, before distorting and turning brown. Head lettuce will have a distorted head or may even fail to form. • Aphids can carry the disease, so you will need to keep an eye on their numbers or buy a disease-resistant cultivar. The infected plant needs to be removed and destroyed. • Other diseases include powdery mildew and white mold.
Swiss Chard	**Insect** • Flea beetles are tiny, glossy brown, green, or black with a similar shape to the cucumber beetles. Although you may not notice the beetles as readily, you will notice the numerous small holes they leave throughout the foliage. • As with most beetles, the best way to protect your crops is to use crop covers and mulch. • Other insects include leafminers and aphids. **Disease** • Cercospora leaf spot starts small with several small brown spots ringed with reddish-purple halos. These spots grow in size until the centers become gray and they fall out. • The infected plant should be removed and destroyed. Increase the airflow by trimming some leaves and then rotating Swiss chard out for a few seasons. • Other diseases include powdery mildew, downy mildew, and bacterial soft rot.

Radish	**Insect**
	• Cabbage root maggot is the bane of most root vegetables. The maggot (larvae with no legs) measures no more than ⅓ inch and feeds on the roots, causing the plant to wilt and die.
	• The adults look similar to the housefly but have a longer and slimmer abdomen. The thorax has gray and black stripes on it.
	• To stop the maggots from getting to your root vegetables, you need to monitor the adults with yellow sticky tape traps and protect crops with row covers. Tilling the soil and rotating crops will also help.
	• Alternatively, grow plants that attract insects that will parasitize and eat the pest.
	• Other insects include cabbage worms and flea beetles.
	Disease
	• Clubfoot is difficult to diagnose until you see the root. The disease starts with the leaves becoming yellow and wilted, causing them to be stunted. Once the root is inspected, it is often swollen and distorted.
	• This is an infectious disease, so clean all tools used. You can also increase the soil pH to 7.2. It is a good idea to rotate radishes out for a while.
	• Other diseases include white rust, radish mosaic virus, and root rot.
Carrots	**Insect**
	• Carrot rust flies are small, black-to-red flies with bulbous red eyes and yellow legs that are tipped black. When at rest, the wings fold neatly over each other.
	• Adults lay eggs on the carrot shoulder (top of the root), and the maggots eat their way through the root, causing rust-colored excrement through their eaten tunnels. The damage will only be noticed after the plant starts to wilt and become stunted.
	• Monitor the adults and add row covers to prevent eggs from being laid on roots. Remove any garden waste which could attract the adults, and consider growing plants that can attract predators and parasitoids. You may also have to rotate crops.
	• Other insects are flea beetles, leafhoppers, and wireworms.
	Disease
	• Aster yellow disease causes carrot tops to discolor and remain short. The root becomes excessively hairy and bitter.
	• This disease is spread by leafhoppers which need to be monitored and controlled. It can also overwinter in garden debris, so ensure to get rid of any infected plants.
	• Other diseases include black canker, leaf blight, and cavity spot.

Basil	**Insect**
	• Whiteflies are small bugs with rounded white wings. They cause damage similar to aphids. The leaves they feed on turn yellow before wilting and dying. They also secrete honeydew, which can attract ants and black sooty mold.
	• The best way to deal with these insects is to increase predatory and parasitoid insects in your garden. You can also spray the affected plant with a quick jet of water to dislodge them. Alternatively, use a small hand vacuum to suck them up.
	• Other insects are aphids, leafhoppers, and flea beetles.
	Disease
	• Fusarium wilt causes yellow spots to develop on leaves on one side of the plant which later turns brown before wilting. This will continue to spread throughout the plant until it is completely infected.
	• The affected plant should be removed and disposed of.
	• Other diseases are powdery mildew, bacterial leaf spot, basil shoot blight, and downy mildew.

PLANTS: PROBLEMS

Each plant you decide to grow has a variety of diseases and pests that can affect it. The best way to treat your plants is to keep a close eye on them while growing and reacting quickly when something seems off.

7

COMMON MISTAKES GARDENERS MAKE AND HOW TO AVOID THEM

I n this final chapter, I will point out mistakes many beginner gardeners tend to make. To avoid the disappointment of your garden not performing the way you want it to, it is advised to consider these points before you do anything.

ENVIRONMENT

Regardless of what garden you want to grow, it needs to be within eyesight. A forgotten garden is a dead garden, or at the very least, one which doesn't thrive. With having a garden in sight, you will spot nuisances before they become problems that require more elbow grease to solve.

When planting outside or deciding to keep containers outdoors, know what your annual first and last frost dates are. These go hand in hand with your hardiness zones. Not knowing these things will jeopardize your garden before it gets a chance to thrive. These aren't the only environmental aspects you need to be concerned about. Never ignore warnings of black frost, hail, or heatwaves. It doesn't take much to protect your plants against these, but if you ignore them, they can destroy your entire garden.

Before laying a raised bed, the soil needs to be adequately prepared, or you will continue to have a problem with weeds growing through the bed. Also, be wary about what you use to fill your raised bed. Many people like to fill it with hay or other grasses to save money. When doing this, ensure that no grass seeds, insects, or diseased material make it into the bed, ruining your healthy soil.

Before placing a raised bed, ensure there are no Homeowners Association (HOA) rules against it. There is nothing worse than doing all the work and then having to destroy it because you failed to abide by the rules of the community.

NEEDS

Consider not only the plant's needs but also your own. Don't bite off more than you can chew. Even though you want to save money by growing your own food, you don't want to spend a lot of money or have a garden you can't manage. Rather start with one raised bed and up to five different plants you want to grow, then several beds and more plants you can eat, give away, or preserve. Start small and grow your skills as a gardener, using what you learned from one growing season and applying it to the next. Then, after you have grown in confidence, you can expand your garden with more raised beds or several containers.

Grow what you like to avoid unnecessary food waste. However, look at different varieties to get some interesting plants you already have a taste for. Avoid spending too much in your first year of gardening, as there is no need for it. Take the time to shop around for deals, upcycle old products to make something new, and keep an eye out for a variety of garden-related items being given away. If you look around, you will be surprised by what you can find.

Plan everything on paper before you pay a cent. During this time, you need to find the ideal location for your garden. Consider the duration of sunlight and if the area has access to water. These are two of the main essentials plants need to thrive. However, plants don't all need the same amounts of the two. Some need more water, while others prefer partial sunlight. Educate yourself about the needs of the plants you want to grow by reading the back of seed packets.

Consider the pros and cons of planting seeds versus planting transplants. Seeds may take longer and require more specialized care, but you're limited with what you can get when buying transplants.

PLANTING CONCERNS

The type of soil you use will determine the quality of what you grow. Never use the soil from a native garden, as you have no idea what can be lurking below the soil. Raised beds need loamy, organic-rich soil, while containers need potting soil with some fertilizer. Don't accept soil from just anywhere. Test the soil to ensure it's within the pH range needed for the plants you want to grow.

Whether you are starting with seeds or transplants, it is vital to space them appropriately. This lowers the chance of competition for resources and the spread of disease. When planting seeds, it is generally encouraged that a few seeds are planted per hole to ensure something sprouts. However, when all manage to sprout, you'll need to thin the seedlings out to prevent competition. Even transplants need to be spaced appropriately. Seed packets have the necessary information about the depth of the seeds that need to be planted and how far apart. For transplants, this information will need to be researched, or ask for assistance from your local garden center.

Even if you get the spacing off a little, it's not a big deal. Many plants can be trimmed back or transplanted to a different part of the garden or into a container. Make notes about the ideal spacing for the next growing season.

Many people get excited about growing a garden and want to plant all the seeds in the packet. Stop! This will only lead to a massive amount of plants and the crops they produce. This causes you to get sick of eating a particular plant, crop waste, or the plants bolting and producing seeds where you don't want them to. The best way to avoid this is to use fewer seeds and stagger the planting of the seeds. By doing this, you have consistent production of crops through the season and not everything ripening at the same time. A little goes a long way, especially with plants that produce through a long growing season. If you want to avoid wastage, teach yourself how to preserve what comes out of your garden or share the bounty.

Although it is better to use organic matter in a raised bed as fertilizer, sometimes this isn't enough. However, if using fertilizer, be wary of using too much. Read the instructions well and know what your plants need to get the most out of the fertilizer.

Mulch is vital if you want to retain moisture levels, suppress the growth of weeds, and prevent pests from getting to plant roots. However, the thickness is important. Too thick and your seedlings won't break through the surface, too thin, and it offers no benefits.

If you notice a problem, deal with it immediately. Weeds that sprout should be uprooted and insects removed. By doing a 30-minute check daily as you water the garden, you will know exactly what is happening to your plants. While moving around the garden, keep an eye on plants producing crops. These crops have a finite life on the plant before they become woody or bitter. Harvest any crops that are ripe to prevent them from becoming inedible. Know what the ripened crop looks like to avoid disappointment. For example, not all varieties of tomatoes are red when they are ripe.

FINAL ADVICE

Educate yourself about different pests and weeds that occur where you live. Once you know what is causing damage to your garden, the easier it becomes to get rid of the problem. Consider which companion plants work well together and which harm other crops. There is a perfect combination to match what you want to grow, you just need to find it.

Don't be afraid to ask for help and advice from people in the neighborhood, your local garden center, and online forums. Gardening is a passion for many, and there are thousands of helpful people willing to share their time-earned experience.

Sometimes it's a good idea to allow some plants to bolt and produce seeds. By saving seeds, you can plant a new garden without having to buy new ones. However, when doing this, be sure you are saving seeds from plants that aren't hybrids. Hybrid plants will grow with many benefits. However, their seeds won't exhibit all the same traits (high yield, insect or disease resistance, etc.) but rather a mixture of the traits. If you want to use the seed from what you are growing, consider starting with heirloom seeds, which are known to have a strong genetic line with specific traits. Avoid using seeds, sets, or bulbs from store-bought plants, as you don't know their origin or if they are even viable.

Lastly, never give up. Gardening is fulfilling, but it isn't instantaneous. It takes time and hard work to get the crops you desire. Use a combination of seeds and transplants, so you don't get discouraged with beds or containers which show no life. Consider growing plants with shorter maturity times with those that take longer. This way, you can be harvesting quick crops while watching the slower-growing crop ripen. Even if your first few seeds and transplants fail, chin up, you have an entire growing season to try again. When the growing season is at an end, turn your attention indoors, and grow whatever you have space for in containers to brighten your diet and home.

CONCLUSION

Gardening is an activity that can be enjoyed by anyone and has a wide range of benefits to health and well-being. The most difficult part of this activity isn't the work you need to put into the soil or getting containers ready but rather the planning. Consider the hardiness zone you are in, how the first and last frost dates affect you, and how much space you have available to determine the type of garden you can have.

Not everyone is lucky enough to have a piece of ground outside to make a raised bed, but many have a sunny spot somewhere in or around their home that is perfect for what plants need. Although some taller plants are best grown in raised beds, you can grow just about anything you want anywhere.

Raised beds allow you to grow above infertile soil, while container gardens allow you to move them to where they will get the most benefits. Don't believe for a minute that you can't grow in a limited space. Think tall, not long, when it comes to vertical gardening.

Each type of garden has pros and cons, and it is up to you to research which will best suit your needs. Once you have decided what will best work for you, think of how you will save on the cost. Consider the time you have to grow outside to choose between seeds or transplants. Then think of what plants you want to grow. All vegetables and herbs grow well outside, while select vegetables and all herbs can benefit from growing indoors or in sheltered areas.

Most vegetables and herbs are considered annuals, but this is only because frost tends to kill most plants during winter. If you plant herbs in containers that can be moved to more sheltered areas during winter, you will find that many are biennials or perennials. You may even find some vegetables last longer than a season when grown indoors.

Why expose your plants to weeds, ground-dwelling insects, and soilborne diseases when you can be growing your plants away from the ground? There are a variety of ways to upcycle or build supports and trellises, which allow for plants to grow upward. This lowers the area the plant takes over (especially those that like to sprawl), increases the duration of sunlight the leaves receive, and allows you to monitor the growing crops at eye level instead of having to bend over to observe them.

Plants are more than just a singular living creature. They work together with others to bring out the best in all of those grown together. Combining a sturdy stalk of corn with climbing beans, support is offered to the beans, while extra nitrogen is supplied to the corn. Companion planting is a great way to utilize the strength of all plants grown together. However, not all plants do well side-by-side, as some prefer more water than others or have invasive roots.

Don't get too comfortable growing the same plants every year in the same spot. This can quickly deplete essential nutrients, and diseases and insects can build up over time. These negative aspects will result in stressed, diseased, and poor-yielding plants. See how yearly crop rotation can aid in the growth of your garden.

Not in the mood to wait weeks to have edible and tasty greens? Gardening is still for you. All you need is a windowsill and a tray of seeds in a growth medium. In a matter of days to a few short weeks, you can have delicious microgreens you can add to any of your meals.

You aren't the only one who wants to enjoy your garden. There is a menagerie of critters that would love to dive into your greens. There's no reason to turn to poisons to persuade these animals to leave your garden alone. Once you can identify the guilty pests, there are a variety of ways of controlling them.

Gardening is a time to experiment and find vegetables, herbs, and microgreens that best suit your needs and tastes. It can also give you those added health benefits that many people lack in their everyday diet. A garden doesn't need to be very big for you to experience the joy that it can bring. Start small and develop it over time. Save the seeds from successful harvests to bring new life to the next growing season. Teach yourself how to create cuttings from herbs and even dry them yourself, so you never have to buy from the store again.

The wonderful world of gardening is at your fingertips. Now that you have all the knowledge needed to start a beginner garden, gardening has never been simpler! Grab a notebook and figure out your hardiness zone and when those tricky frost dates are. Then pick your favorite vegetables, herbs, and microgreens. Guaranteed, there is an ideal spot somewhere in your garden or home that would make the perfect start to your garden. You better go find it and start planning so that you can get your garden going. What are you waiting for? The growing season is only so long, and there are fresh vegetables, herbs, and microgreens just waiting to come to life with your hard work.

REFERENCES

Anderson, T. (2020, February 6). *Don't make these 15 common garden mistakes.* Lovely Greens. https://lovelygreens.com/15-mistakes-beginner-gardeners-allotment/

Andrychowicz, A. (2018, April 11). *How to build a raised garden bed with concrete blocks – complete guide.* Get Busy Gardening. https://getbusygardening.com/concrete-block-raised-bed/

Andrychowicz, A. (2022, February 28). *How to make a cattle panel trellis arch.* Get Busy Gardening. https://getbusygardening.com/cattle-panel-trellis-diy/

Beaulieu, D. (2019, September 16). *Weed control without chemicals.* The Spruce. https://www.thespruce.com/weed-control-without-chemicals-2132928

Boeckmann, C. (2019, July 28). *Broccoli.* Old Farmer's Almanac. https://www.almanac.com/plant/broccoli

Bonnie Plants. (n.d.). *9 common mistakes of new gardeners and how to avoid them.* https://bonnieplants.com/blogs/garden-fundamentals/9-mistakes-new-gardeners-make-and-how-to-avoid-them/

Chadwick, P. (2021, March). *How to grow, harvest, and preserve culinary herbs.* Piedmont Master Gardeners. https://piedmontmastergardeners.org/article/how-to-grow-harvest-and-preserve-culinary-herbs/

Chase, A. R. (2014, April 25). 10 ways to keep your garden healthy. *Fine Gardening.* https://www.finegardening.com/article/10-ways-to-keep-your-garden-healthy

Chinn, L. (2018, December 19). *How to get rid of aphids & whiteflies on basil.* Home Guides. https://homeguides.sfgate.com/rid-aphids-whiteflies-basil-24584.html

Di Gioia, F. (2020, May 11). *A step-by-step guide for growing microgreens at home.* Penn State Extension.https://extension.psu.edu/a-step-by-step-guide-for-growing-microgreens-at-home

ECO gardener. (2018, September 21). *The basics of vegetable gardening for beginners.* https://ecogardener.com/blogs/news/the-basics-of-vegetable-gardening-for-beginners

Farmer, D. (2022, May 25). *Vegetable container gardening ideas for indoor or outdoor gardening.* Dian Farmer Learning to Grow Our Own Food. https://dianfarmer.com/vegetable-container-gardening-ideas-for-indoor-or-outdoor-gardening/

Felman, A. (2020, July 30). *Gardening 101: What to know to actually see your garden grow.* Greatist. https://greatist.com/connect/beginners-guide-to-gardening

GardenTabs. (2021, April 13). *15 ideas for recycled planters for your vertical garden.* https://gardentabs.com/recycled-planters/

Giles, S. (2021, May 21). *Best vegetables to grow in raised beds: 15 easy and rewarding crops for your garden.* Gardeningetc. https://www.gardeningetc.com/us/advice/best-vegetables-to-grow-in-raised-beds

Gill, L. L., & Christian, T. (2021, November 9). *Your guide to growing, drying, and storing herbs and spices.* Consumer Reports. https://www.consumerreports.org/gardening-landscaping/diy-guide-to-growing-drying-storing-herbs-and-spices/

GrowVeg. (2021, March 7). *Vegetable crop rotation made simple - our rainbow system* [Video]. YouTube. https://www.youtube.com/watch?v=64YapgN6G2w

Hess, A., & Hamilton, M. (2014, December 18). *10 tips for a naturally bug-free garden.* Mother Earth News. https://www.motherearthnews.com/organic-gardening/10-tips-for-a-naturally-bug-free-garden-zbcz1412/

Hobby Farms. (2012, August 6). *10 beginning gardener mistakes to avoid.* https://www.hobbyfarms.com/10-beginning-gardener-mistakes-to-avoid-2/

IOL. (2020, September 25). *10 surprising health benefits of gardening.* https://www.iol.co.za/lifestyle/health/10-surprising-health-benefits-of-gardening-128a5e25-09c1-41ac-a526-786fe9672d2e

LaLiberte, K. (2022, January 18). *Keeping animal pests out of your garden.*

Gardener's Supply. https://www.gardeners.com/how-to/keep-animals-out-of-your-garden/5426.html

Lamp'l, J. (2018, March 8). *042-Raised bed gardening, pt. 1: Getting started.* Joe Gardener. https://joegardener.com/podcast/raised-bed-garden ing-pt-1/

Madore, J. D. (n.d.). *How much depth & space do potatoes need to grow? (3 things to know).* GreenUpSide. https://greenupside.com/how-much-depth-and-space-do-potatoes-need-to-grow/

Marine, M. (2021, May 5). *Grow up this year with vertical garden planters: Ideas, tips, & tricks.* Simplify, Live, Love. https://simplifylivelove. com/grow-up-this-year-with-vertical-garden-planters-ideas-tips-tricks/

Michaels, K. (2022, February 9). *Vegetable container gardening for beginners.* The Spruce. https://www.thespruce.com/vegetable-container-gardening-for-beginners-848161

Miracle-Gro. (n.d.). *10 top gardening tips for beginners.* https://www.mira clegro.com/en-us/library/gardening-basics/10-top-gardening-tips-beginners

Neverman, L. (2020, January 18). *Raised garden beds – 5 tips for surefire success.* Common Sense Home. https://commonsensehome.com/raised-garden-beds/

Neverman, L. (2021, March 16). *How to start a garden – 10 steps to gardening for beginners.* Common Sense Home. https://common sensehome.com/start-a-garden/

Old Farmer's Almanac. (2022a, May 26). *Vertical gardening: Grow more vegetables in less space.* https://www.almanac.com/vertical-garden ing-grow-more-vegetables-less-space

Old Farmer's Almanac. (2022b, June 23). *13 common garden weeds.* https://www.almanac.com/content/common-garden-weeds

Savannah H. (2015, May 18). *Growing, preserving and mixing your own herbs and spices (part 1).* Off the Grid News. https://www.offthegrid news.com/survival-gardening-2/growing-preserving-and-mixing-your-own-herbs-and-spices-part-1/

Singer, F. (2019, July 2). *Microgreens 101: How to grow microgreens at home.* Herbs at Home. https://herbsathome.co/how-to-grow-micro greens-at-home/

Sweetser, R. (2022, June 15). *Container gardening: Growing vegetables in pots.* Old Farmer's Almanac. https://www.almanac.com/content/container-gardening-vegetables

The Editors. (2018, November 23). *Beans.* Old Farmer's Almanac. https://www.almanac.com/plant/beans

The Editors. (2019a, February 16). *Bell peppers.* Old Farmer's Almanac. https://www.almanac.com/plant/bell-peppers

The Editors. (2019b, March 28). *Carrots.* Old Farmer's Almanac. https://www.almanac.com/plant/carrots

The Editors. (2019c, April 4). *Lettuce.* Old Farmer's Almanac. https://www.almanac.com/plant/lettuce

The Editors. (2019d, April 22). *Chives.* Old Farmer's Almanac. https://www.almanac.com/plant/chives

The Editors. (2019e, May 19). *Tomatoes.* Old Farmer's Almanac. https://www.almanac.com/plant/tomatoes

The Editors. (2019f, June 11). *Cucumbers.* Old Farmer's Almanac. https://www.almanac.com/plant/cucumbers

The Editors. (2019g, July 4). *Radishes.* Old Farmer's Almanac. https://www.almanac.com/plant/radishes

The Editors. (2019h, July 28). *Parsley.* Old Farmer's Almanac. https://www.almanac.com/plant/parsley

The Editors. (2019i, September 2). *Basil.* Old Farmer's Almanac. https://www.almanac.com/plant/basil

The Editors. (2019j, September 27). *Mint.* Old Farmer's Almanac. https://www.almanac.com/plant/mint

The Editors. (2022, February 22). *Building trellises and supports for climbing vegetables.* Old Farmer's Almanac. https://www.almanac.com/video/building-trellises-and-supports-climbing-vegetables

The Editors. (n.d.-a). *Rosemary.* Old Farmer's Almanac. https://www.almanac.com/plant/rosemary

The Editors. (n.d.-b). *Sage.* Old Farmer's Almanac. https://www.almanac.com/plant/sage

The Editors. (n.d.-c). *Swiss chard*. Old Farmer's Almanac. https://www. almanac.com/plant/swiss-chard

The Editors. (n.d.-d). *Zucchini*. Old Farmer's Almanac. https://www. almanac.com/plant/zucchini

The Gardening Channel With James Prigioni. (2019, October 3). *How to build a raised bed cheap and easy backyard gardening* [Video]. YouTube. https://www.youtube.com/watch?v=MBIYebUgVVI

TIMG. (2021, February 18). *How and when to fertilize vegetable plants in gardens, raised beds & containers*. This Is My Garden. https://thisismy garden.com/2019/05/fertilize-vegetable-plants/

Tukua, D. (2022, June 6). *22 ways to combat garden pests naturally*. Farmers' Almanac. https://www.farmersalmanac.com/combat-garden-pests-naturally-20886

Urban Eden. (2018, March 2). *Organic weed control & the importance of weeding*. Urban Eden Landscaping. https://www.lawncarecamas. com/blog/importance-of-weeding/

USDA. (2020). *USDA plant hardiness zone map*. https://planthardiness. ars.usda.gov/

Vanderlinden, C. (2022, April 12). *Grow your own microgreens*. The Spruce. https://www.thespruce.com/grow-your-own-micro greens-2540008

Vegetable Gardening Online. (n.d.). *Indoor container gardening tips and ideas*. http://www.vegetable-gardening-online.com/indoor-container-gardening.html

VermiBag Composting & Gardening Systems. (2018, April 7). *VermiBag Ep 23 "Making a raised bed garden with concrete blocks"* [Video]. YouTube. https://www.youtube.com/watch?v=k9nL8YLpjEk

Victoria. (2020, March 15). *Simple DIY raised garden beds*. A Modern Homestead. https://www.amodernhomestead.com/simple-diy-raised-garden-beds/

IMAGE REFERENCES

Alleksana. (2020, May 29). *Close-up photo of garlic near herbs.* Pexels. https://www.pexels.com/photo/close-up-photo-of-garlic-near-herbs-4113891/

Congerdesign. (2015, August 21). *Flower decoration garden lavender snapdragons.* Pixabay. https://pixabay.com/photos/flower-decoration-garden-lavender-896205/

Ehlers, M. (2020, April 4). *Close-up photo of green leaves.* Pexels. https://www.pexels.com/photo/close-up-photo-of-green-leaves-3816343/

Göllner, A. (2019, August 8). *Raised bed chili chives garden herbs nature.* Pixabay. https://pixabay.com/photos/raised-bed-chili-chives-garden-4392783/

Hoffman, G. (2021, May 1). *Unrecognizable farmer planting sprouts in countryside.* Pexels. https://www.pexels.com/photo/unrecognizable-farmer-planting-sprouts-in-countryside-7728077/

Kampus Production. (2021, April 27). *An elderly man in a vegetable garden.* Pexels. https://www.pexels.com/photo/an-elderly-man-in-a-vegetable-garden-7658811/

Kireva, D. (2021, October 15). *Brown rat on the grass.* Pexels. https://www.pexels.com/photo/brown-rat-on-the-grass-9783103/

Krukove, Y. (2020, October 19). *Ball pepper growing in garden.* Pexels. https://www.pexels.com/photo/ball-peppers-growing-in-garden-5479384/

Lisa. (2020, April 15). *Person holding a red radish.* Pexels. https://www.pexels.com/photo/person-holding-a-red-radish-plant-4039451/

Malkova, O. (2021, August 2). *Sweet pea on white background.* Pexels. https://www.pexels.com/photo/sweet-pea-on-white-background-9031150/

Nitra, A. (n.d.) *Colourful plants and cacti line the front of a house photo.* Burst. https://burst.shopify.com/photos/colourful-plants-and-cacti-line-the-front-of-a-house?q=plants+inside

Pixabay. (2017, August 7). *Yellow bee on white flower on selective focus photography.* Pexels. https://www.pexels.com/photo/yellow-bee-on-white-flower-on-selective-focus-photography-60579/

Roseclay, D. (2019, July 23). *Green leafed plant.* Pexels. https://www.pexels.com/photo/green-leafed-plant-2686987/

Sarangi, B. (2014, March 31). *Ridge gourd turai vine trellis climber vegetable.* Pixabay. https://pixabay.com/photos/ridge-gourd-turai-vine-trellis-300912/

Sbaynham. (2019, September 17). *Herbs nature natural dried herbs tea plants.* Pixabay. https://pixabay.com/photos/herbs-nature-natural-dried-herbs-4481005/

Smith, D. (2016, February 15). *Hornworm nature insect caterpillar larva garden.* Pixabay. https://pixabay.com/photos/hornworm-nature-insect-caterpillar-1198377/

Stebnicki, M. (2019, May 9). *Piles of assorted varieties of vegetables.* Pexels. https://www.pexels.com/photo/pile-of-assorted-varieties-of-vegetables-2255935

Summa. (2017, June 22) *Work in the garden garden digging plucking weeds.* Pixabay. https://pixabay.com/photos/work-in-the-garden-garden-digging-2432111/

Wei, W. (2018, December 6). *Six potted plants close-up photo.* Pexels. https://www.pexels.com/photo/six-potted-plants-close-up-photo-1660533/

WikimediaImages. (2015, July 16). *Amaranthus retroflexus redroot pigweed.* Pixabay. https://pixabay.com/photos/amaranthus-retroflexus-844463/

www.ingramcontent.com/pod-product-compliance
Lightning Source LLC
Chambersburg PA
CBHW060524130626
46553CB00002B/641